THE KINGFISHER FACTS AND RECORDS BOOK OF SPACE

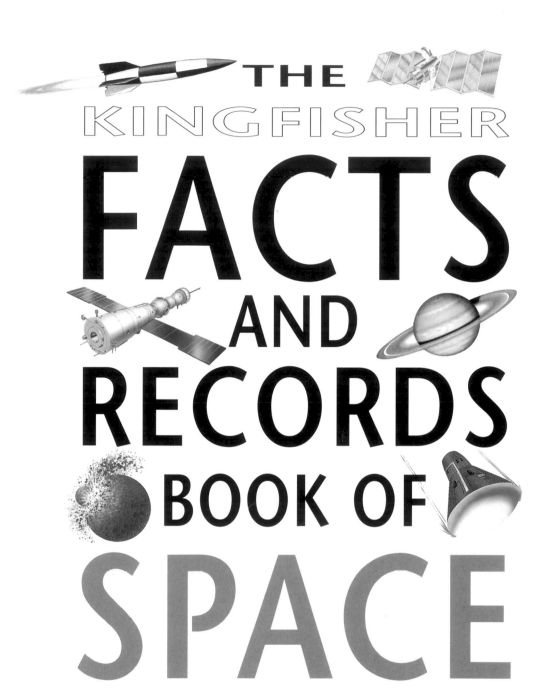

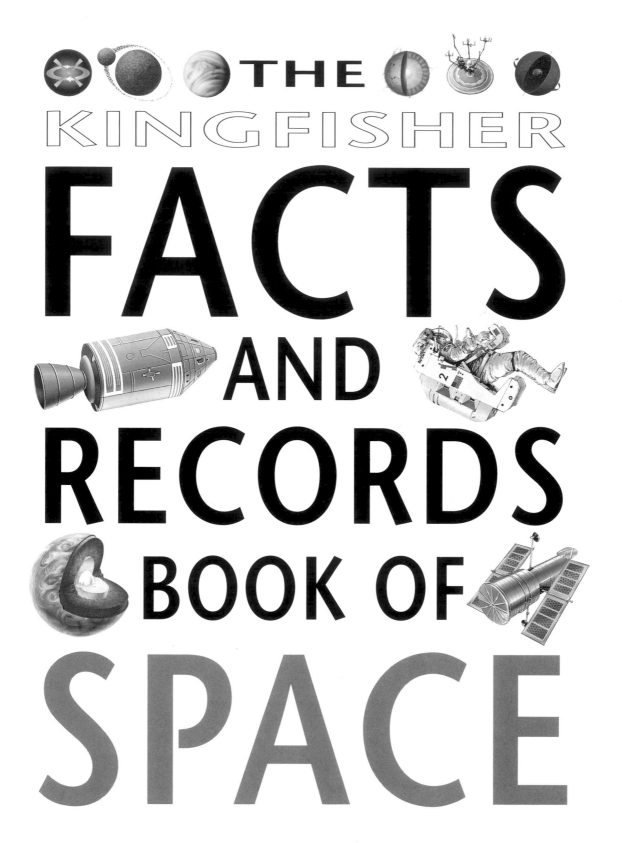

THE KINGFISHER FACTS AND RECORDS BOOK OF SPACE

KING*f*ISHER

Author	Clive Gifford
Deputy Art Director	Mike Buckley
Art Editor	Keith Davis
Designer	Joe Conneally
Editors	Fergus Collins, Clive Wilson
Picture Researcher	Tara McCormack
DTP Co-ordinator	Nicky Studdart
Production Controller	Jacquie Horner, Caroline Hansell
Artwork Archivists	Wendy Alison, Steve Robinson
Indexer	Sue Lightfoot

KINGFISHER
Kingfisher Publications Plc
New Penderel House, 283–288 High Holborn
London WC1V 7HZ
www.kingfisherpub.com

Produced by Scintilla Editorial
33 Great Portland Street
London W1W 8QG

First published by Kingfisher Publications Plc 2001
1 3 5 7 9 10 8 6 4 2
1TR/0201/TWP/MAR/SMA150

Copyright © Kingfisher Publications 2001

A CIP catalogue record for this book is available from the British Library.

ISBN 0 7534 0542 8

Printed in Singapore

CONTENTS

SOLAR SYSTEM

SUN AND STARS

UNIVERSE

SKYWATCHING

PEOPLE AND SPACE

THE FUTURE

SOLAR SYSTEM

The Solar System is made up of nine planets, over 60 moons and millions of asteroids and comets. At its centre is the largest object in the system, the Sun. It is the Sun's huge gravitational pull that holds the Solar System together and controls the movement of the planets.

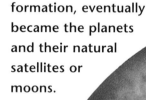 Birth of a star system

Astronomers believe that the Sun formed around five billion years ago from a huge cloud of gas and dust called the solar nebula. As the solar nebula began to shrink, it pulled in more and more gas and dust into its centre, became hotter and started to form a central orb surrounded by a spinning disc of gas and dust. Nuclear processes (see page 24) within the central orb started up, eventually becoming the Sun we rely on today for heat and light. Much of the material in the disc, left over from the Sun's formation, eventually became the planets and their natural satellites or moons.

Between Mars and Jupiter are a large number of rocks called asteroids. These form the asteroid belt.

BORN FROM DUST
In (1), the Solar System is a spinning cloud of dust. Gravity within the cloud pulls matter towards the centre (2), where nuclear reactions create our embryonic Sun. The rest of the dust spins around the central Sun (3), coming together to form the nine orbiting planets, (4).

A spherical region of comets called the Oort Cloud surrounds the Solar System.

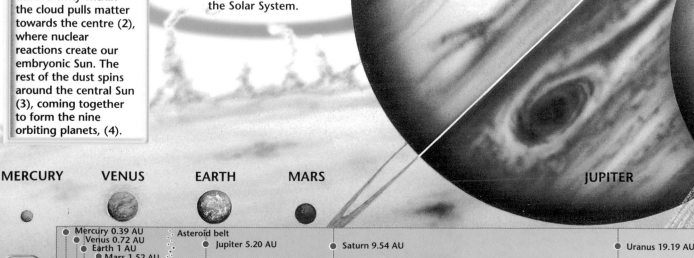

MERCURY   VENUS   EARTH   MARS   JUPITER

Mercury 0.39 AU
Venus 0.72 AU
Earth 1 AU
Mars 1.52 AU
Asteroid belt
Jupiter 5.20 AU
Saturn 9.54 AU
Uranus 19.19 AU

Planetary motion

Each planet turns slowly on its axis. A complete 360° turn is called a planet's rotational period or day. It takes Earth just over 23 hours, 56 minutes to complete a rotation. Planets travel around the Sun along a path called an orbit. The time taken to complete one orbit is known as an orbital period or year. Each planet has a different orbital period. The further it is from the Sun, the longer the orbit. For centuries, orbits were thought to be circular. We now know that all planets travel in oval, or elliptical orbits, at times closer to the Sun, at others farther away. The point at which a planet is furthest from the Sun is called aphelion. When it is nearest to the Sun it is said to be at perihelion.

In 1995, a planet was discovered in another star system for the first time. It is 150 times bigger than Earth.

Measuring distances

Astronomers use a special unit of measurement to represent the huge distances involved in the Solar System and Universe. The distance between stars is measured in light years. Light travels about 300,000km every second. In a light year, it journeys around 9.46 million million km. Within the Solar System, the basic unit of distance is the Astronomical Unit (AU). This is the average distance Earth lies away from the Sun – 149,600,000km. Neptune, for example, is 30 AUs away from the Sun – that is 30 times farther from the Sun than Earth.

Of the planets, Venus has the most circular orbit and Pluto the most elliptical.

DATABANK

INPUT

Q How big is the Solar System?

Q Is our star system the only place in the Universe that has planets?

Q What's the difference between a planet and a moon?

OUTPUT

A The Solar System fills an area approximately 15 trillion km in diameter.

A Astronomers have recently discovered as many as 50 planets in other solar systems.

A A planet is a body that orbits a star. A moon or natural satellite is an object that orbits a planet.

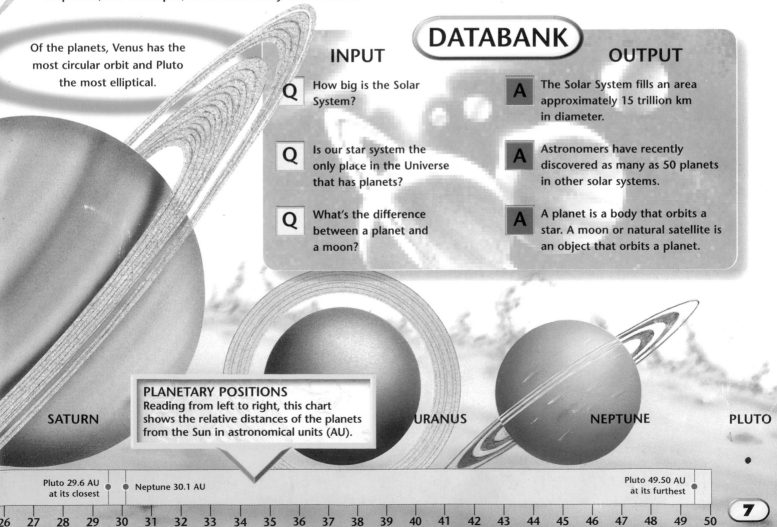

PLANETARY POSITIONS
Reading from left to right, this chart shows the relative distances of the planets from the Sun in astronomical units (AU).

SATURN — URANUS — NEPTUNE — PLUTO

Pluto 29.6 AU at its closest | Neptune 30.1 AU | Pluto 49.50 AU at its furthest

26 27 28 29 30 31 32 33 34 35 36 37 38 39 40 41 42 43 44 45 46 47 48 49 50

EARTH AND ITS MOON

The third planet from the Sun, Earth is the only place where life is known to exist. This is partly because it is just the right distance from the Sun, which prevents Earth's water from being boiled away or permanently frozen.

Atmosphere: extends 500km into space

Mantle: 3,000km thick

Outer core: 2,200km thick

Inner Core: 2,500km in diameter

Crust: 7–35km thick

Earth's structure

The fifth largest planet in the Solar System, Earth is larger than the three other rocky inner planets – Mercury, Venus and Mars. Beneath its solid crust lies a hot, rocky layer known as the mantle. This is solid but can move like ice in a glacier. The crust is formed from 15 plates, which float on the mantle. Beneath the mantle lies the outer core. Made of molten iron, this generates Earth's powerful magnetic field. The inner core is solid iron.

FIERY FURNACE
The temperature at Earth's core may reach 6,200°C. Heat rises through the mantle in convection currents.

Earth's surface area is 510 million sq km. The Moon's surface area is about 38 million sq km.

FACTS AND FIGURES

Earth's diameter at the equator is 12,756km. Its circumference at the equator is 40,075km.

The Moon is a cold place with an average temperature of -20°C. The temperature can drop as low as -153°C.

The largest crater on the Moon is called Hertzsprung and has a diameter of 591km.

If Earth's ice melted, the sea levels would rise by 100m. As it is, only 30 per cent of Earth's surface is land.

HOT BEGINNINGS
Earth formed five billion years ago from matter left over from the Sun's creation. Initially hot, it cooled and shrank over time.

As Earth cooled and condensed, it became the densest planet in the entire Solar System.

While Earth is on average about 149,600 million km from the Sun, the Moon is 384,400km from Earth.

Harbouring life

From space, Earth's blue colour, its white polar caps and wispy atmosphere mark the planet out as something special. With its moderate temperature range and average surface temperature of 15°C, Earth allows liquid water to exist in huge quantities on its surface. Water is essential to life, as is the gas oxygen. Earth's atmosphere, which extends up more than 100km from its surface, is made up of 21 per cent oxygen, 77 per cent nitrogen and small amounts of argon, water vapour, carbon dioxide and other gases.

Earth's four main oceans, the Atlantic, Pacific, Indian and Arctic, hold 97.2 per cent of Earth's total water.

LIVING PLANET
Seen from the Moon, Earth's atmosphere seems very thin and fragile. Astronauts report being greatly moved by the sight.

LUNAR EXPLORATIONS
This map shows the face of the Moon that is visible from Earth and marks the landing sites of the six Apollo missions.

Lunar surface

A rocky, pitted place, the Moon is a quarter of the size of Earth. Large lava plains called *maria* form most of the side of the moon we can see. Of its 1,940 named features, 1,545 are craters created mainly by asteroids crashing into its surface. The Moon has no atmosphere, winds or flowing water to erode its surface. What we see there has remained unchanged for three or four billion years.

With no atmosphere to carry sound vibrations, the Moon is a completely silent place.

MOON FORMATION
The Moon may have formed from debris expelled into orbit around Earth by a collision between Earth and a huge object.

Sea of Showers

Sea of Serenity

Apollo 15

Apollo 17

Sea of Crises

Ocean of Storms

Sea of Tranquillity

Sea of Clouds

Apollo 11

Apollo 12

Sea of Fertility

Apollo 14

Apollo 16

Sea of Nectar

Sea of Moisture

NEAR SIDE OF THE MOON

HORIZON
As the Moon is so much smaller than Earth, horizons appear closer to the observer than they do on Earth.

Phases of the Moon

In its orbit around Earth, the Moon always shows the same side to us. The far side is often called the dark side because it cannot be viewed from Earth. The way the Sun's light hits the surface of the Moon makes it appear to change shape within its monthly orbit. These different shapes are called phases, and there are five main types: new, crescent, quarter, gibbous and full. When the Moon is new and dark to us, the far side is lit by sunshine. We think of Earth's gravity keeping the Moon in orbit around our planet, but the Moon pulls back, too. It's the Moon's pull that creates the sea and ocean tides.

MOONSHINE
At New Moon, the unlit side of the Moon faces Earth so it seems invisible. At Full Moon we see the whole sunlit face.

Sunlight

Sunlight

Last quarter

Waning gibbous

Full Moon

Waning crescent

Waxing gibbous

New Moon

Earth

First quarter

Waxing crescent

MERCURY AND VENUS

Mercury and Venus are the two planets closest to the Sun. Both are made of solid rock, are warmer than Earth and neither has moons. Yet probes have proved that they are extraordinarily different from each other.

Caloris Basin

FACTS AND FIGURES

A day on Venus lasts 117 Earth days. A year on the hostile planet lasts just 225 Earth days.

Mercury's average distance from the Sun is 57.9 million km, while Venus is 108.2 million km from the Sun.

Mercury has the shortest year in the Solar System – 88 Earth days. The planet's year is half as long as its day.

Of the planets, only Venus and Uranus rotate east to west. On Venus, you would see the Sun rise in the West.

From radar maps it is thought that 80 per cent of Venus' surface is covered in dusty lava plains.

Mercury has 297 named features. 239 of these are craters.

All bar one of the 1,761 named features on Venus bear a female name.

Mapping Mercury

Caught up in the Sun's glare Mercury is hard to examine from Earth. Most of what we know about the planet comes from the *Mariner 10* mission of 1974–75. The probe's thousands of photographs showed a dead world, full of craters and solidified lava flows. The craters are believed to have been created more than four billion years ago when debris left over from the formation of the Solar System crashed into the planet.

Mercury has a wrinkled surface. This may be because its cooling iron core caused the planet to shrink.

HOLE PUNCH
The Caloris Basin is a 1,300km-wide crater made when an object at least 100km in diameter collided with Mercury.

Temperature extremes

The Sun's strong gravitational pull has slowed Mercury's rotation so much that the planet's day lasts 176 Earth days. This, along with the almost non-existent atmosphere, gives the planet's surface time to become fiercely hot when facing the sun. It also allows the surface to cool to well below freezing when it is in shadow. The temperature extremes on Mercury have been measured at -173°C at its coldest and 427°C at its hottest.

MARINER 10
Mariner 10 discovered that Mercury has a weak magnetic field, produced by the planet's large core.

BIG SUN
The Sun, when viewed from the surface of Mercury, appears 6.3 times brighter than it does from Earth.

DATABANK

Q Has a probe ever landed on Mercury and, if not, how close has one flown to the surface?

A The *Mariner 10* probe flew as close as 756km to the planet's surface during its 1975 mission.

Q Have any probes actually landed on the surface of Venus?

A Four Russian Venera probes have landed and sent back photographs and data.

Earth's twin?

Named after the Roman goddess of beauty,
Venus is the brightest planet visible from Earth. Separated from Earth by just
42 million km and almost the same size, Venus is sometimes referred to as
Earth's twin. Such a name can be deceiving because Venus is a desolate rocky
waste, hostile to life. With a surface
temperature of around 480°C, the
planet is hotter than Mercury
– despite being further
from the Sun. Its surface,
mapped by radar, is
largely the result of
volcanic activity.

Venus is known as the morning or
evening star as it only appears just after
sunset or just before sunrise.

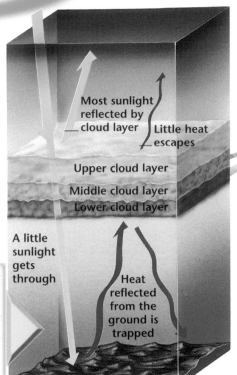

Most sunlight
reflected by
cloud layer | Little heat
escapes

Upper cloud layer

Middle cloud layer

Lower cloud layer

A little
sunlight
gets
through

Heat
reflected
from the
ground is
trapped

SIZE COMPARISON
Venus is 12,104km wide while
Mercury has a diameter of just
4,879km. By comparison our
Moon's diameter is 3,476km.

SMOG WORLD
The thick layer of
carbon dioxide
cloud acts as a
blanket, stopping
most of the Sun's
heat from
getting away.

Heavy atmosphere

Venus is cloaked in a thick, choking blanket of carbon dioxide.
Only about 20 per cent of the sunlight that strikes Venus reaches
the ground yet the planet has an incredibly high surface temperature.
This is the result of the heavy atmosphere trapping in the heat, creating what is called the Greenhouse Effect.
The atmosphere also presses down hard on the planet's surface. The pressure is similar to
being underwater on Earth at a depth of 914m. Large clouds within the atmosphere rain
sulphuric acid onto the planet's surface. Scientists believe
that if it were possible to land on Venus,
the sky would appear
a gloomy orange.

FIRE AND BRIMSTONE
Volcanic reactions on Venus have sent vast
amounts of sulphur into the atmosphere.
These form acidic clouds.

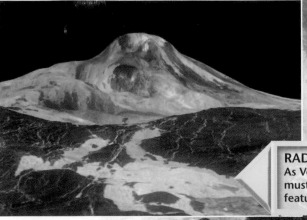

RADAR MAP
As Venus' atmosphere is so thick, radar
must be used to build up a picture of its
features such as the mountain Maat Mons.

MARS

Named after the Roman god of war, Mars is the only planet whose surface is visible – through the aid of a telescope – from Earth. It is also the least hostile planet and may even once have supported life.

The red planet

The fourth planet from the Sun, Mars is about half the size of Earth with a diameter of just 6,787km. It is approximately one and a half times further from the Sun than Earth. Its orbit around the Sun is highly elliptical (oval-shaped) and its distance from the Sun varies by up to 40 million km. Half of its surface shows signs of past volcanic activity with many volcanoes and what may have been lava-flow channels scouring its rocky, desert-like surface. Mars remains tilted on its axis in a similar way to Earth as it orbits the Sun. This gives it similar seasons to those on Earth although Martian seasons are almost twice as long.

POLAR ICE CAP
Mars' ice caps appear to grow in winter and recede in summer. The northern ice cap is three times the size of the southern.

SCARRED PLANET
At 4,000km long and reaching 5–10km deep, the Valles Marineris is the largest canyon system in the Solar System.

OLYMPUS MONS
About 600km in diameter and with a crater 90km wide, Mars' giant volcano is the largest in the Solar System.

DATABANK

INPUT	OUTPUT
Q Are there really irrigation channels on Mars?	**A** No, the channels were possibly made by ancient rivers.
Q Does Mars have an atmosphere like Earth's?	**A** No. It is 95 per cent carbon dioxide and 0.03 per cent oxygen.
Q What makes Mars red? Is the planet going rusty?	**A** Yes! Iron in the soil reacts with oxygen creating iron oxide.
Q When did the first mission to Mars occur?	**A** In 1962, the Soviet Union sent the *Mars-1* probe.

Moons of Mars

Mars has two irregular-shaped moons, Phobos and Deimos. These may have once been asteroids, which were caught in the planet's gravity. Both moons were discovered by astronomer Asaph Hall in August 1877. He named them after the sons of the god of war in Greek Mythology. Phobos orbits Mars in only seven and a half hours. Its month is a third the length of a Martian day.

Deimos

Phobos

Life on Mars?

From ancient times until the 20th century, people have thought that life might exist on the red planet. Early astronomers believed the darker areas of Mars' surface were lush vegetation and, in Victorian times, some notable astronomers claimed to see straight lines etched on the planet's surface, which they believed to be irrigation channels. The data collected by orbiting probes and landers paints a less romantic picture.

Mars does not appear to contain any form of life. Its thin atmosphere, with only 1 per cent of the atmospheric pressure of Earth, contains almost no water, does little to keep the average temperature well below freezing and does not shield the surface from lethal doses of ultraviolet rays. Debate does continue, however, on whether Mars supported life millions of years ago.

About 4 billion years ago, Mars may have been warm enough for rivers and oceans to flow over its surface.

Future unmanned missions to Mars may try and grow bacteria or manufacture fuel on the planet.

FACTS AND FIGURES

The closest Mars gets to the Sun is 206 million km. The nearest it passes to Earth is about 56 million km away.

A Martian day, known as a sol, lasts 24 hours 37 minutes while a year lasts 687 Earth days.

Mars' surface temperature averages -63°C but varies from an icy -128°C to a pleasant 27°C.

In 1971, *Mariner 9* orbited Mars successfully and took 7,329 photographs of the planet's surface.

Phobos orbits Mars at an average distance of just 5,982km. Its largest crater, Stickney, is 10km across.

Deimos is so small and its gravity so weak that a speed of only 36 km/h is needed to escape its gravity.

Just 15km long, Deimos orbits at over 23,000km from Mars. It is the second smallest moon in the Solar System.

At times, Mars appears as the third brightest object in the night sky, after Venus and the Moon.

SURVEYOR
Global surveyor reached Mars in 1997 and orbited as close as 350km from the surface during its 18-month-long mission. It mapped the planet and its weather in incredible detail.

WATER PROBE
Scientists have built probes to test below Mars' surface. The Russian *Mars 96* mission carried the *Penetrator* (above), which had a 6m-long probe. Sadly, the *Mars 96* craft exploded on the launchpad.

GENTLER PLANET
Despite lacking water and a breathable atmosphere, Mars' environment is not as hostile as other rocky planets', like Venus.

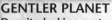

JUPITER

The giant of our Solar System, Jupiter is the fifth planet from the Sun, and is 1,300 times bigger than Earth. Its mass is more than two and a half times the total of all the other planets combined.

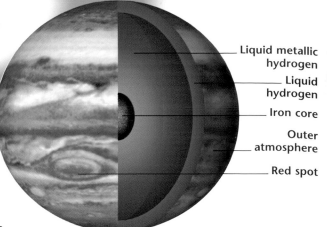

- Liquid metallic hydrogen
- Liquid hydrogen
- Iron core
- Outer atmosphere
- Red spot

 ## Jupiter's structure

Jupiter is a gas giant with a gravity 2.7 times as strong as Earth's. Around 90 per cent of the planet is made of hydrogen, with helium making up almost all of the remainder. Jupiter's outer layers are hydrogen and helium gas. Below this, massive pressure forces the two gases to act more like a liquid metal. Here, powerful magnetic fields are generated, strong enough to send out radio waves that can be picked up on Earth. The planet's core is thought to be compressed rock and iron. Scientists have discovered that Jupiter is shrinking. This process helps to generate the extreme temperatures found at the core, which astronomers estimate to be as high as 30,000°C.

Jupiter has a thin ring circling it. Although not as impressive as Saturn's rings, it is 30km thick and 6,500km wide.

ME AND MY SHADOW
Taken by the *Hubble Space Telescope*, this photograph shows the moon Io – and its shadow – orbiting Jupiter.

 ## Moons of Jupiter

So far, sixteen moons have been located around Jupiter. The four largest, Io, Europa, Ganymede and Callisto, are known together as the Galilean Moons after the Italian astronomer Galileo. He was the first to examine them with a telescope, in 1610. Ganymede is the Solar System's largest moon. At 5,268km in diameter, it is larger than the planets Mercury and Pluto. Io is the most volcanically active body in the Solar System. Its volcanoes send plumes of gas up to 250km high. The smallest of Jupiter's moons is Leda. With a diameter of only 8km across, it's the smallest moon of all the nine planets.

EASILY SPOTTED
Jupiter's four largest moons, Io, Ganymede, Europa and Callisto, can be seen from Earth by using a telescope.

Europa

Callisto

Ganymede

Io

HOT WHEN PULLED
The gravities of Jupiter, Ganymede and Europa play tug-of-war with Io, heating the moon up so that its interior is molten.

DATABANK

INPUT	OUTPUT
Q Who first measured Jupiter and when did this occur?	**A** British astronomer James Bradley first measured it in 1733.
Q When did scientists find out that Jupiter had rings like Saturn?	**A** In 1979, the *Voyager 1* probe made a fly-by of the giant planet.
Q Why are scientists so interested in Jupiter's moon, Europa?	**A** There is a chance that life could exist under Europa's icy surface.
Q How big is Jupiter in comparison to the Sun?	**A** Jupiter is just one thousandth of the Sun's mass.

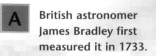

Fast spinner

For such a huge planet, Jupiter spins incredibly fast, completing its day in under ten hours. At the equator, the speed of rotation is 45,259.5 km/h – more than 25 times as fast as Earth. The huge forces created by this speed make Jupiter bulge out an extra 9,000km at its equator. Jupiter's turning speed along with the heat rising from the planet's core – which is hotter than the Sun's surface – generate its unusual weather patterns. Violent storms whip across much of its surface, stretching clouds out into bands parallel with the equator. Where the different bands of cloud meet, especially violent storm systems develop. Some of the largest are visible by telescope from Earth, such as the Great Red Spot.

In 1994, fragments of the comet Shoemaker-Levy 9 smashed into Jupiter, leaving huge dark marks.

GUSTY GIANT
The *Galileo* orbiter dropped a probe into Jupiter's gassy atmosphere in 1995. This probe measured the winds blowing through the atmosphere at a ferocious but fairly constant 531 km/h.

FACTS AND FIGURES

Jupiter's average distance from the Sun is 778.33 million km. It takes 11 years, 315 days to make one orbit.

NASA's *Galileo* probe reached Jupiter in 1995. It made 10 orbits of the planet, which took a total of 22 months.

Jupiter's magnetic field is 20,000 times stronger than Earth's, and may stretch 1.6 million km from the planet.

The moon Callisto is covered with craters. It consists of 60 per cent rock and iron and 40 per cent ice and water.

Sinope orbits Jupiter at a distance of 23.7 million km – the largest orbit of any of the Solar System's moons.

The colour of the Great Red Spot may be due to compounds of phosphorus or sulphur, but no one is sure.

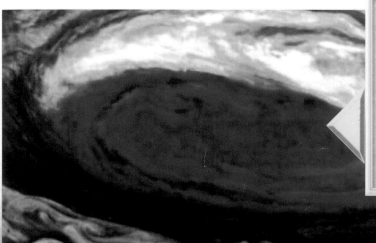

NASTY SPOT
Jupiter's Great Red Spot is an enormous hurricane that has been raging for the last 300 years. Two to three times the diameter of Earth, the spot rotates anti-clockwise once every six days. Winds blow throughout this vast area at speeds of around 450 km/h.

SATURN

The ringed planet is the sixth from the Sun, and the second largest after Jupiter. It is the flattest planet in the Solar System due to its exceptionally high rotation speed.

Saturn has such a low density that if it were possible to immerse it in water, it would float.

 ## A rock and gas giant

The composition of Saturn has long been something of a mystery. Once thought to be formed entirely of gas, this giant planet is now believed to have a rocky core at its centre. This core, estimated at between 20,000 and 30,000km across, is surrounded by a shell of metallic liquid hydrogen that helps generate Saturn's magnetic field. Liquid hydrogen extends out from the centre for thousands of kilometres. This is surrounded by Saturn's atmosphere, which is made up mainly of hydrogen and helium.

FACTS AND FIGURES

Saturn's average distance from the Sun is 1.43 billion km. It takes 29.46 Earth years to orbit the Sun.

At its equator, Saturn's diameter is 120,536 km, while at its poles the diameter is 109,119km.

Saturn has circulating bands of clouds. The planet's fastest winds race at up to 1,800 km/h.

On Saturn the Sun appears one per cent as bright as it does on Earth. The average temperature is an icy -120°C.

Pan is Saturn's tiniest moon. At just 20km in diameter, it is smaller than many asteroids.

COMET TALE
Saturn's rings may have formed from a comet that strayed into the planet's gravitational field.

 ## The rings

Galileo first observed something strange about Saturn in 1610, but his telescope was weak and he thought Saturn was a triple planet. Then, in 1655, Christiaan Huygens confirmed the existence of the now familiar rings. Scientists have since identified over 10,000 separate rings, each made up of millions of tiny particles of rock and ice, arranged in bands of different density.

DISAPPEARING
Every 14 or 15 years, Saturn's rings turn edge-on to Earth, and disappear. With the glare from the rings gone, it becomes easier to see Saturn's other features. Thirteen of Saturn's moons were discovered during such times.

Although over 250,000km in diameter, Saturn's rings are no more than 30km thick.

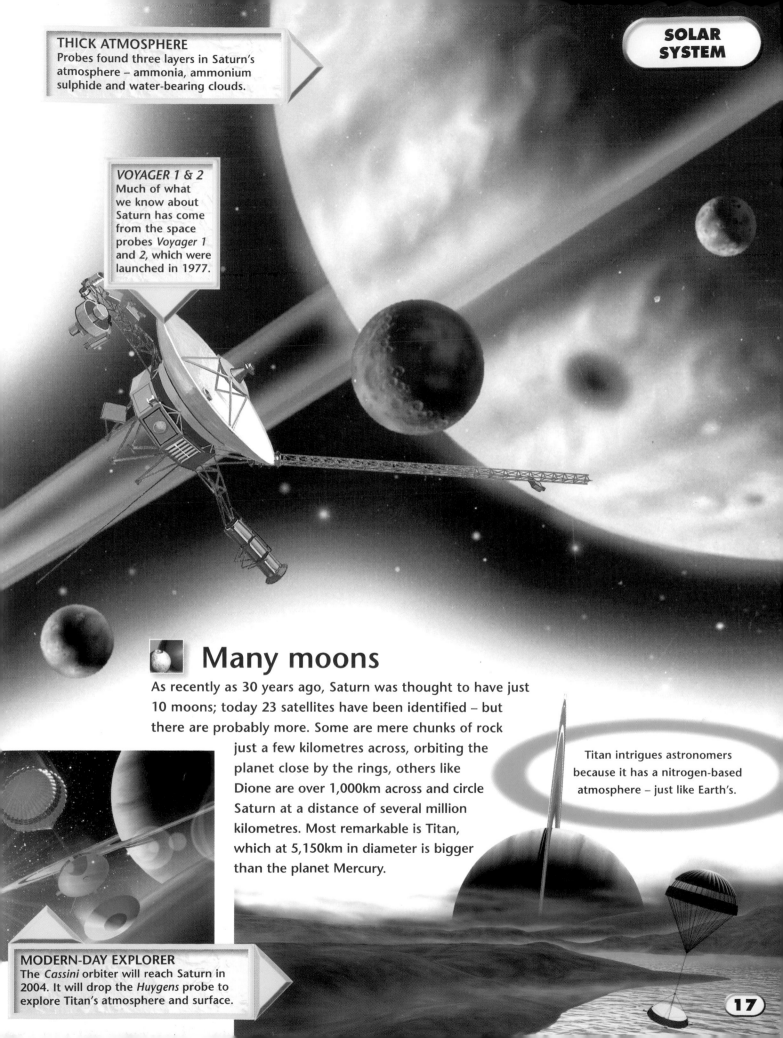

THICK ATMOSPHERE
Probes found three layers in Saturn's atmosphere – ammonia, ammonium sulphide and water-bearing clouds.

VOYAGER 1 & 2
Much of what we know about Saturn has come from the space probes *Voyager 1* and *2*, which were launched in 1977.

Many moons

As recently as 30 years ago, Saturn was thought to have just 10 moons; today 23 satellites have been identified – but there are probably more. Some are mere chunks of rock just a few kilometres across, orbiting the planet close by the rings, others like Dione are over 1,000km across and circle Saturn at a distance of several million kilometres. Most remarkable is Titan, which at 5,150km in diameter is bigger than the planet Mercury.

Titan intrigues astronomers because it has a nitrogen-based atmosphere – just like Earth's.

MODERN-DAY EXPLORER
The *Cassini* orbiter will reach Saturn in 2004. It will drop the *Huygens* probe to explore Titan's atmosphere and surface.

THE OUTER PLANETS

Lying many millions of kilometres away, Uranus, Neptune and Pluto were unknown until powerful telescopes were developed. Over the last 25 years, probes have given us further tantalising glimpses of these distant worlds.

Uranus

Uranus travels around the Sun an average of 2,870 million km away. Its interior is thought to consist of a tiny rocky core surrounded by clouds of methane ice. Beyond this, the planet's outer layers are composed of hydrogen and helium gas. Uranus boasts 15 moons, the largest reaching 145km in diameter and the smallest just 26km across. These are all named after characters in English literature. Uranus' rings were first found in 1977. A decade later, *Voyager 2* detected a total of 11 rings made of very dark rocks and a little ice or dust.

Twice as far away from us as Saturn, Uranus appears as a tiny green disc when viewed through a telescope.

Voyager 2

Our knowledge of Uranus and Neptune was sketchy until the triumphant *Voyager 2* mission. Launched in 1977, *Voyager 2* journeyed past Jupiter in 1979, Saturn in 1981, Uranus in 1986 and Neptune in 1989. *Voyager 2* made a large number of discoveries including six of Neptune's moons and nine moons around Uranus – all were new to astronomers. The probe also mapped details of the planets, such as Neptune's fierce winds and the rings that surround Uranus.

EXPLORER
Voyager 2 used nuclear power instead of solar panels to provide fuel. The craft featured 16 small rocket thrusters, which were used to correct its course as it journeyed to the far reaches of the Solar System.

ON EDGE
Uranus appears to lie on its side so that one pole and then the other faces the Sun on the planet's long orbit.

FACTS AND FIGURES

Uranus was first discovered by the astronomer William Herschel in 1781. At first he thought it might be a comet.

Uranus is 51,000km in diameter. Its day is 17 hours and 14 minutes long. Its year takes 84 Earth years.

Neptune is 49,500km in diameter. Its day is 16 hours and 7 minutes long while a year takes 165 Earth years.

Neptune was discovered to be a planet by Johann Galle in 1846 due to the way its gravity affected Uranus' orbit.

William Herschel originally wanted to name Uranus after the English king, George III, but he was overruled.

Pluto's diameter is 2,250km. Its day lasts 6 days and 9 hours. Its year lasts 248 Earth years.

The average temperature on Pluto is thought to be about -230°C although this varies during the planet's orbit.

TRITON
Neptune's biggest moon, Triton is the Solar System's coldest land surface with a temperature of -235°C.

CHURNING SPOT
The Great Black Spot in Neptune's hydrogen, helium and methane atmosphere is large enough to swallow Earth.

Neptune

Neptune orbits the Sun an average of 4,497 million km away. The temperature of its atmosphere is estimated at -210°C. Like Uranus, it has rings, although Neptune's five or more rings are faint compared to those of its neighbour. Neptune has eight moons, the largest of which, Triton, is especially interesting. It is 2,076km across and has a crust made of rock-hard ice. Plumes of nitrogen gas regularly erupt from the surface like geysers. Other moons include Proteus and Nereid.

Neptune appears blue from space because methane in its atmosphere absorbs red light.

Pluto

The American astronomer Clyde Tombaugh discovered Pluto in 1930. About a tenth of the size of Earth, Pluto is relatively unknown as no telescope has seen it clearly. We do know that Pluto has one moon, called Charon, which is half the size of the planet it orbits. Pluto has an eccentric orbit that carries it as close as 4,425 million km from the Sun and as far away as 7,375 million km. This means that for 20 years in every 250, Pluto moves inside Neptune's orbit and Neptune becomes the outermost planet.

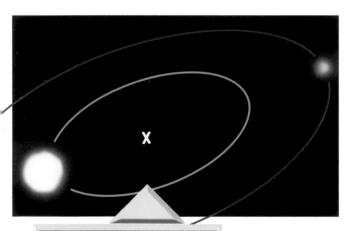

X

SPACE WALTZ
Pluto and its moon Charon orbit each other around a centre of gravity (X). They always show each other the same face.

ROCKY OUTPOST
Pluto may have a rocky core surrounded by layers of ice and frozen methane. It could once have been a moon of Neptune.

PLUTO AND CHARON
If you were to stand on the surface of Pluto, the moon Charon would seem very large – seven times the size of our Moon.

COMETS AND OTHER BODIES

Planets, moons and the Sun are not the only bodies in the Solar system. Asteroids form a large belt between Mars and Jupiter. Comets orbit the Sun at great distances and can sometimes be seen from Earth. Meteors and meteorites are rocks that enter Earth's atmosphere.

 ## Asteroids

Asteroids are chunks of rock, metal or a combination of the two, which orbit the Sun. Over 90 per cent of all the Solar System's asteroids lie in the 344 million km-wide asteroid belt that is found between Mars and Jupiter. This doughnut-shaped body of objects is believed to be the remains of a planet that never properly formed when the Solar System was in its infancy. Larger asteroids are sometimes referred to as the minor planets. Ceres, the first asteroid to be discovered, is also the largest with a diameter of about 1,000km. Vesta, the third largest asteroid, is the only member of the belt close enough and large enough to be seen with the naked eye.

SPACE ROCKS
The asteroid Ida (left) is one of the thousands of large objects (above) that make up the asteroid belt. Ida orbits the Sun just like a tiny planet, and even has its own miniature moon – called Dactyl.

Over 200,000 tonnes of space rock enters Earth's atmosphere every year and over 3,000 meteorites land.

 ## Meteors and meteorites

Meteors are small pieces of rock and dust that enter Earth's atmosphere. Most are fragments of asteroids but some are small pieces of debris from Mars, the Moon or comets. Most meteors burn up in the atmosphere, forming streaks of light in the night sky called shooting stars. Some larger chunks of debris do not burn up completely and impact on Earth's surface. These are called meteorites. Most meteorites are made of rock although some are made of iron or a mixture of rock and iron. All are eagerly sought by collectors.

SURVIVAL OF THE BIGGEST
The vast majority of meteors burn up about 50km above the ground. Large ones occasionally make it through to strike Earth.

DATABANK

Q Do we have evidence that anyone has been killed by a meteorite?

A No, although a dog in Nakhla, Eqypt, was struck dead by one in 1911.

Q When will Halley's Comet next be seen?

A It passed closest to Earth in the 1980s and will be back in the 2050s.

BOLT FROM THE BLUE
Many people believe that a meteorite impact changed Earth's climate and wiped out the dinosaurs 65 million years ago.

STREAKER
When you look at a comet in the night sky, it does not appear to be moving much but may be travelling at over 160,000 km/h.

CLOSE-UP
In the nucleus of a comet, jets of gas escape from the surface and are blown by the solar wind to form a tail.

Comets

Comets are like huge, dirty snowballs that orbit the Sun. The head of a comet contains a nucleus just a few kilometres across made up of rocky dust bound in ice. As a comet gets closer to the Sun, some of the ice melts releasing dust. This forms a glowing head, called a coma, and a tail. Comets are divided into short and long-period comets based on how long they take to complete an orbit around the Sun. A short period comet is one whose orbit takes less than 200 years. A comet is usually named after the person who discovered it. The most famous was discovered in 1682 by astronomer Edmund Halley. He predicted the comet's return every 76 years.

In 1983, the comet IRAS-Araki-Alcock passed within 5 million km of Earth – one of the closest on record.

FACTS AND FIGURES

Although many orbit close to Earth, asteroids are thought to strike Earth only once every 250,000 years.

The biggest meteorite found on Earth – in Namibia, Africa – measured 2.7m by 2.4m and weighed 60 tonnes.

The largest known comet was the Great Comet of 1811. Its coma was estimated at 1.8 million km wide.

The Great Comet of 1843 possessed a tail long enough to wrap round the Earth's equator 8,000 times.

An estimated 10 trillion comets lie at the edge of the Solar System making up what is called the Oort Cloud.

Comets are less dense than water or air. If all the comets were combined, they would weigh little more than Earth.

Comet Encke takes just three years to orbit the Sun while other comets may take many thousands of years.

BACK AGAIN
Halley's Comet is recorded many times in history, such as when it appeared over Jerusalem in AD66 (far left). Halley noticed a pattern in the records, from which he predicted when the comet would next appear.

STARS AND STAR TYPES

On a clear night, you can see over 2,500 faint pinpricks of light dotted across the night sky – just a fraction of the billions of stars that exist in the Universe. Stars come in many sizes and burn with a surprising variety of brightnesses.

 ## Measuring brightness

How bright a star appears from Earth – its apparent magnitude – is not a guide to how brightly it shines throughout the Universe. So astronomers use a scale called absolute magnitude, which is a measure of a star's brightness if viewed from a distance of 32.6 light years. The smaller the magnitude number, the brighter the star.

The dimmest stars yet observed have absolute magnitudes of over 18 while the brightest stars have magnitudes of -8 or less. Each whole number step on the magnitude scale equals an increase or decrease in brightness of 2.5 times. This means that a star of the first magnitude is 100 times brighter than a star of the sixth magnitude – the faintest stars visible to the naked eye.

LITTLE AND LARGE
Betelgeuse (right) is a giant, but tiny G1623b (with its larger companion below) is just a tenth of the mass of our Sun.

TWINKLE, TWINKLE, LITTLE STAR
A star may appear to twinkle because air movement in Earth's atmosphere makes the light from the star twist and bend.

The *Hipparcos* probe, launched in 1989 by the European Space Agency, accurately measures star positions.

FACTS AND FIGURES

The use of magnitude for measuring a star's brightness was devised in 130BC by Hipparchus of Nicaea.

A star with an apparent magnitude of 9 is the faintest star observable from Earth using binoculars.

The smallest star so far observed is called UV Ceti B. It has a mass of only 3.5 per cent of the Sun.

The brightest object in the night sky (except the Moon) is the planet Venus with an apparent magnitude of -4.

If Betelgeuse replaced our Sun in the Solar System, its outer atmosphere would extend past Jupiter.

 ## Binary stars

Many stars do not exist alone like our Sun. Instead they belong to a star system, which contains two or more stars. Binary star systems with two stars account for about a fifth of all stars so far observed. In some binary star systems, the two may be extremely close, orbiting each other in a few hours. In other systems, the stars may be many millions of kilometres apart. Binary stars interest astronomers because, by measuring the effect of each star's gravity on the other, it is possible to calculate each one's mass.

NEIGHBOURS
Although binary stars appear to revolve around each other, they are really orbiting a common centre of gravity (X).

The measures of a star's brightness shown here are absolute magnitudes.

CAPELLA
About 1,200 light years away, this type G appears as the sixth brightest star. Its magnitude is 0.4.

BETELGEUSE
This type M star is 310 light years away and has a magnitude of -7.2. Its size makes it seem even brighter.

OUR SUN
Our own local star is a type G star, which means that it is not particularly hot – in relation to other stars.

VEGA
Just 25 light years away, Vega is a type A star, one of the brightest stars we can see, with a magnitude of 0.6.

Temperature and colour

Stars are classified in many ways, from their size and position to their colour. A star's colour usually depends on its temperature. The hottest stars glow blue-white and the coolest stars are an orange-red colour. Astronomers divide nearly all stars up into seven classes of what they call spectral types, depending on their temperature. These run from type O, the hottest, through types B, A, F, G, K to type M, the coolest. The Sun is a type G star.

ARCTURUS
Arcturus is an orange giant and is classed as a type K star. It is 36 light years away and has a magnitude of 0.2.

While most stars are too far away to yield detail, scientists have found a bright patch on Betelgeuse's surface.

- ● Type O
- ● Type B
- ○ Type A
- ○ Type F
- ○ Type G
- ● Type K
- ● Type M

This chart shows the basic star types from O (the hottest) to M (the coolest).

SIRIUS
This type A star appears bright because it is just 8.6 light years away. However, its absolute magnitude is only 1.4.

DATABANK

Q What is the most distant star so far observed by astronomers?

A A supernova in the galaxy AC 118 was found to be 5,000 million light years away.

Q Which star has the greatest absolute magnitude in our galaxy, the Milky Way?

A Cygnus OB2 number 12 has an absolute magnitude of approximately -10.

RIGEL
A massive blue variable star, Rigel is classed as a type B. It is 900 light years away and has a magnitude of -8.1.

ALDEBARAN
The orange-red giant Aldebaran is 68 light years from us. A type K star, it shines with a magnitude of -0.3.

THE SUN

The Sun is the Solar System's power station, generating vast amounts of heat and light energy. In the scale of the Universe, the Sun is not particularly large or powerful, but it is the only star scientists have been able to study in detail.

 ## Structure

Like all stars, the Sun is a huge ball of hot gas. Probes and other research show that it has an incredibly hot core where the energy is generated. The energy passes through the radiative zone around the core and out into the next layer, the convective zone. The Sun's surface is called the photosphere. It is about 400–500km thick and consists of constantly churning gases. The Sun's inner atmosphere is called the chromosphere. It is approximately 9,600km deep and ranges in temperature from 4,000°C at the bottom to over 50,000°C at the top. Above the chromosphere is the Sun's outer atmosphere called the corona – a glowing halo that extends for several million kilometres into space.

In 1998, NASA sent the *TRACE* probe to study the Sun's corona and photosphere.

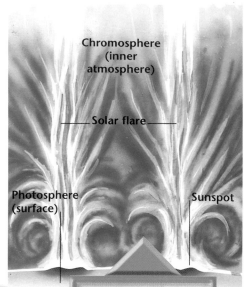

Solar flare bursts above corona (outer atmosphere)

Chromosphere (inner atmosphere)

Solar flare

Photosphere (surface)

Sunspot

SOLAR FLARE
A solar flare is a violent explosion over a sunspot that sends huge amounts of radiation into space.

Solar furnace

The Sun's energy is generated at its core. Extremely high temperatures create nuclear fusion where the nuclei (core particles) of hydrogen atoms collide and form helium atoms, releasing vast amounts of energy in the process. More than 600 million tonnes of hydrogen are converted into helium every second. The core's temperature rages at 15 million°C. Light and heat energy flow out from the core in waves through the radiative zone and into the convective zone. There, violent churning motions throw the energy out to the visible surface of the Sun and then on into space.

STRUCTURE
The Sun is made up of several layers of different temperatures. At its centre is the nuclear furnace that makes up its core. While only 2 per cent of the Sun's volume, the core accounts for 60 per cent of its mass.

Photosphere

Photosphere (Sun's surface)

Convective zone

Radiative zone

Core or solar interior

Radiative zone

Convective zone

Sunspot

The Sun blasts out seven million tonnes of material every second. This stream of particles is called the solar wind.

DATABANK

Q Is radiation from the Sun dangerous to us?

A Yes. Luckily, ozone in our atmosphere prevents most radiation from reaching Earth.

Q What is a sunspot?

A A dark area on the surface of the Sun, which is slightly cooler than the rest of the planet.

ULYSSES
The space probe *Ulysses*, launched in 1990, studies the solar wind and the magnetic field above the Sun's poles.

Solar eclipses

An eclipse is when one planet or satellite blocks out some or all of another. A solar eclipse occurs when the Moon's orbit takes it in front of the Earth blocking part or all of the Sun from view for a short period. Sometimes the Moon only covers part of the Sun – this is called a partial eclipse. Total eclipses are rarer, and only a narrow stretch of the Earth's surface sees the sun blocked out completely. The total eclipse of August 1999 occupied a 100km-wide corridor stretching from the northern Atlantic Ocean across southwestern England, central Europe and on into the Middle East and India. Eclipses in 2001 and 2002 will both occur in southern Africa.

When the Moon is at its greatest distance from Earth, it is too small to cover the Sun completely during an eclipse.

FACTS AND FIGURES

The Sun's diameter is 1.4 million km. It makes one rotation every 25.4 Earth days.

The Sun's mass is 330,000 times greater than Earth's. Its core is about 27 times bigger than the Earth.

The number of sunspots rises and falls in eleven year cycles. The spots move from the poles to the centre.

The Sun is about 5 billion years old. It will continue to shine for another 5 billion before it starts to die.

The Sun's outer layer consists of 73 per cent hydrogen gas, 25 per cent helium and 2 per cent other elements.

Just one square centimetre of the Sun's surface shines with the brightness of over 230,000 candles.

DIAMOND
For just a few seconds either side of a total eclipse, a sudden gleam of bright light appears between the mountains of the Moon. This stunning sight is referred to as the diamond ring.

GRADES OF SHADOW
During an eclipse, the Moon casts a shadow with a dark centre, the umbra, surrounded by a lighter area, the penumbra.

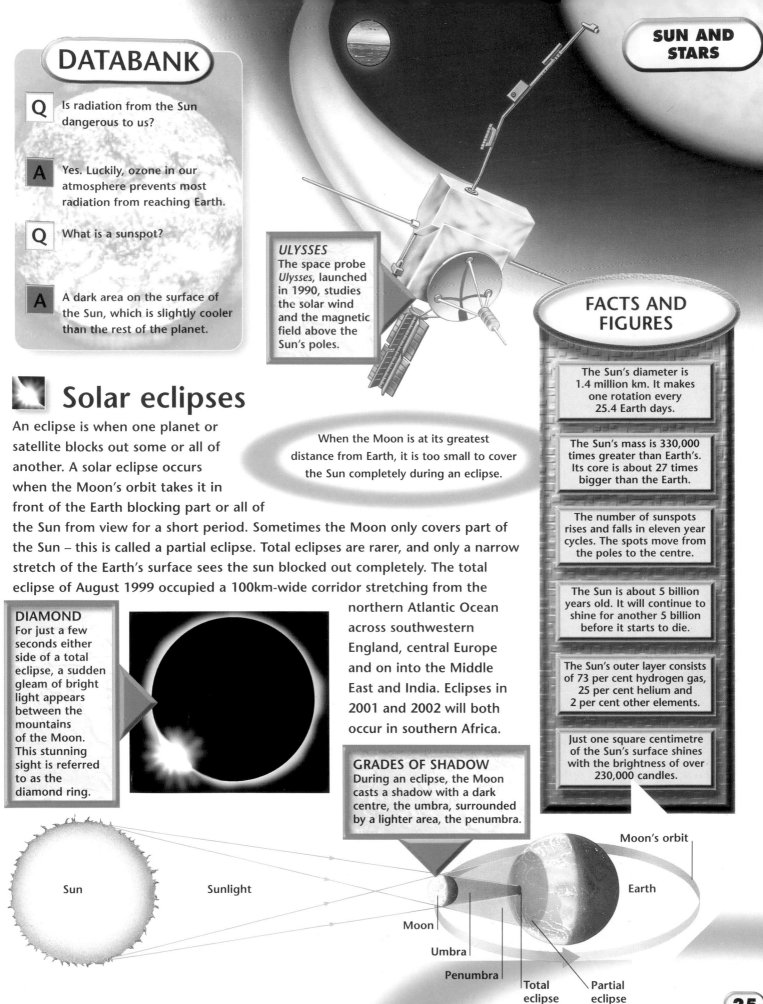

Sun

Sunlight

Moon's orbit

Earth

Moon

Umbra

Penumbra

Total eclipse

Partial eclipse

BIRTH AND LIFE OF STARS

Just like people, stars are born, live and die. The difference is that a star's lifespan is measured in billions of years. New stars are being born all the time, and scientists are beginning to understand just how.

The cloud of dust and gas found within a nebula may sometimes be the remains of a dead star.

Star birth

Most stars are born within a huge cloud of gas and dust called a nebula. Space holds millions of nebulae, and they can be observed from Earth when they reflect light from nearby stars. Stars are born when forces within the nebula, such as the pull of the gas's gravity or a shockwave caused by a nearby star explosion, make the cloud of gas and dust shrink and grow hotter. As it does so, it breaks up into smaller clumps, each of which may eventually form a star.

Protostars

As the clumps of gas shrink, they form what astronomers call a protostar. This is a baby star that has yet to start generating energy in its core by nuclear fusion. The shrinking cloud of gas starts to spin round faster and faster. As its spin speed increases, it becomes a disc shape. The centre, or core, of the protostar gets increasingly dense and hot until nuclear fusion is finally triggered. The energy produced helps to blow much of the disc of gas away, leaving the new star shining brightly.

CAUGHT IN THE ACT
This pillar of gas and dust is part of the vast Eagle Nebula. Baby stars emerge from the tips at the edge of the cloud.

OUT OF DUST
Here a cloud of gas and dust breaks from the main nebula. Slowly, the knot of matter gathers together in a disc. As the disc spins it heats up until a nuclear reaction takes place – a new star Is born.

Nebula
– a swirling cloud of dust and gas

A dense knot of gas and dust breaks away

FACTS AND FIGURES

The Orion Nebula is over 50 light years across. Scientists have found more than 150 protostars within it.

Algol is an eclipsing variable star where an eclipse occurs once every 2.9 days and lasts for ten hours.

Eta Carinae is an eruptive variable star first discovered in 1677 by English astronomer, Edmund Halley.

The first drawing of a nebula was made by Dutch astronomer Christiaan Huygens in 1656.

Mira is a pulsating variable star, which shines at magnitudes that vary between 2.0 and 10.1.

One of the youngest known stars is IRAS4. Astronomers believe it is thousands rather than millions of years old.

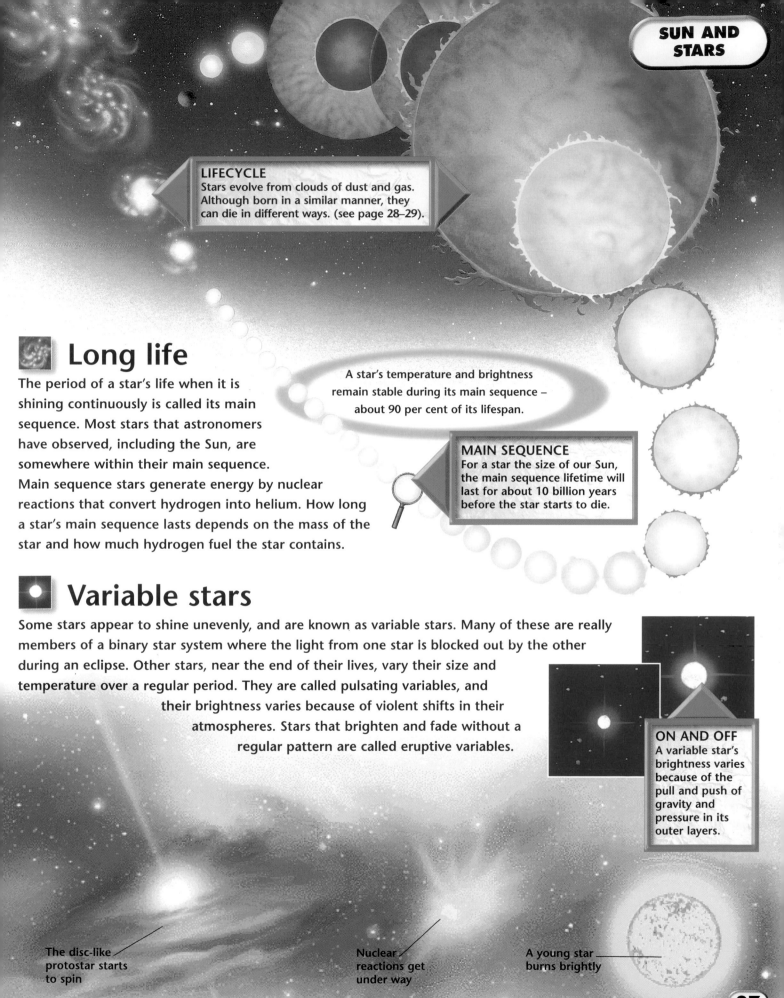

LIFECYCLE
Stars evolve from clouds of dust and gas. Although born in a similar manner, they can die in different ways. (see page 28–29).

Long life

The period of a star's life when it is shining continuously is called its main sequence. Most stars that astronomers have observed, including the Sun, are somewhere within their main sequence. Main sequence stars generate energy by nuclear reactions that convert hydrogen into helium. How long a star's main sequence lasts depends on the mass of the star and how much hydrogen fuel the star contains.

A star's temperature and brightness remain stable during its main sequence – about 90 per cent of its lifespan.

MAIN SEQUENCE
For a star the size of our Sun, the main sequence lifetime will last for about 10 billion years before the star starts to die.

Variable stars

Some stars appear to shine unevenly, and are known as variable stars. Many of these are really members of a binary star system where the light from one star is blocked out by the other during an eclipse. Other stars, near the end of their lives, vary their size and temperature over a regular period. They are called pulsating variables, and their brightness varies because of violent shifts in their atmospheres. Stars that brighten and fade without a regular pattern are called eruptive variables.

ON AND OFF
A variable star's brightness varies because of the pull and push of gravity and pressure in its outer layers.

The disc-like protostar starts to spin

Nuclear reactions get under way

A young star burns brightly

DEATH OF STARS

A star may exist for billions of years but it will not last forever. Eventually, it starts to die. Stars die in a variety of ways and leave behind different legacies, from red giants and white dwarfs to incredibly dense black holes or cataclysmic explosions.

The beginning of the end

For most stars, the end comes when they begin to use up their hydrogen fuel. A small star such as our Sun then swells up to become a red giant. Its core continues to burn, using helium as fuel. The burning helium casts off the red giant's outer atmosphere, which becomes what is called a planetary nebula. The star cools and condenses to become a white dwarf star, which shines until its last heat radiates away. Stars much larger than our Sun contract after they use up their fuel, and absorb all the energy instead of giving it off. As the energy is exhausted, the star is ripped apart by a spectacular explosion called a supernova.

When a star explodes in a supernova, it shines more brightly than all the other stars in the galaxy put together.

RED GIANT
At maximum size, a red giant is up to 1000 times the size of our Sun. However, its dense core may only be the size of Earth.

CINDERS
Over billions of years, a white dwarf cools. Eventually it will shrink to a dark cinder and no longer produces light.

Neutrons and black holes

When a massive star dies, its heavy core may become a neutron star. These are the smallest and densest stars yet found. Neutron stars are made when enormous forces compress the star's atoms, forcing protons and electrons in the atoms to make a solid ball of neutrons. Some stars collapse further, and disappear into an amazingly dense point called a singularity. A black hole is the space around a singularity. Scientists cannot see a black hole but they can detect one through its effects.

A black hole is the densest object in the Universe. Its gravitational pull is so massive even light cannot escape.

FACTS AND FIGURES

The first 10 seconds of a supernova produce 100 times more energy than our Sun generates in 10 billion years.

If Earth was compressed into solid neutrons, like a neutron star, it would be a ball only 60m in diameter.

A pinhead of solid neutrons would weigh at least as much as two enormous supertanker ships.

When the Sun becomes a red giant, it will swell in size to about 30 times its present diameter.

The gas swirling towards a black hole heats up to temperatures as high as 100 million °C.

GIANT STAR DEATH
Blue giants are among the largest and hottest stars in the Universe. When they run out of fuel, they usually explode.

SPINNING TOP
Pulsars spin at different speeds but astronomers believe they will all gradually slow down as they run out of energy.

Pulsars

Radio astronomer, Jocelyn Bell thought she may have discovered signals from an extraterrestrial intelligence when she monitored a regular series of radio pulses received by the Cambridge radio telescope in 1967. What the British scientist had encountered was a pulsar, a rapidly spinning neutron star. Pulsars send out light and radio waves as beams of energy as the star spins round. If Earth is in the path of the beam, then the pulsar's beam appears to blink on and off, like a rotating lighthouse light. Most pulsars flash between five times a second and once every two seconds.

Over 700 pulsars have so far been discovered. The slowest spinners take over 5 seconds to complete a revolution.

GAS THIEF
Many stars come in pairs. If one star dies and collapses into a black hole, it may drag in gas from the other. As the living star's gas spirals into the black hole, it gives off x-rays, which can reach Earth.

INTERGALACTIC FLASHER
As a pulsar spins, escaping electrons are channelled by the star's massive magnetic field into a beam of radiation and light.

GIVE-AWAY
Scientists study the x-rays given off by a black hole's activity in order to locate the hole's exact position in space.

DATABANK

INPUT	OUTPUT
Q What is the speed of the fastest spinning pulsar yet found?	**A** In 1982, experts found a pulsar that spins 642 times a second.
Q Where do scientists think the nearest black hole to Earth is?	**A** There may be a black hole within our own galaxy, the Milky Way.
Q Will our own Sun die and if so, when will it happen?	**A** Yes, it will start to run out of hydrogen in about 5 billion years.
Q Could a human possibly travel in and out of a black hole?	**A** As far as scientists can tell, nothing escapes from a black hole.

EXPANDING UNIVERSE

The Universe consists of space and everything within it. It is unbelievably huge and appears to be getting bigger. There are many ideas as to how the Universe was born but the most widely accepted among scientists is the Big Bang theory.

IN THE BEGINNING
The Big Bang created enough energy to make all the matter in the Universe. The Universe then began to expand.

EARLY DAYS
As the swiftly expanding Universe cooled, the forces that governed it, such as gravity and nuclear forces, separated out. Atoms did not form for at least 300,000 years after the Big Bang.

The Big Bang

The Big Bang theory suggests that the entire Universe started more than 12 billion years ago. It began in a minute point when some form of gigantic explosion started the process of forming matter, time and space. No one knows what caused the Big Bang but it is believed that the explosion was followed by cosmic inflation in which incredible forces were generated. In the smallest fraction of a second, the Universe grew from smaller than an atom to bigger than a galaxy. Since then it has continued to expand rapidly.

OUT OF NOTHINGNESS
The Big Bang occurred within the tiniest fraction of time. Nothing existed before it – not even time or space.

FACTS AND FIGURES

Edwin Hubble discovered the Universe was expanding in 1929. The Hubble Space Telescope is named after him.

The idea of the Big Bang was first detailed by Belgian priest Bernard Lemaître in the 1920s.

The Big Bang explosion would have generated temperatures in excess of 10,000 trillion trillion°C.

The communications satellite *Telstar* was the first device to detect possible radiation left over from the Big Bang.

The phrase 'Big Bang' was coined by the British astronomer Fred Hoyle in a radio programme.

Spaced out

Launched in 1990, the *Cosmic Background Explorer* found signs of the Big Bang in the Universe's background radiation.

Through much research, we have learnt that the Universe is becoming larger and larger every day. Three billion years ago, for example, galaxy clusters were 25 per cent closer than they are today. Although the Universe is increasing in size, it is not expanding into anything. Space itself is expanding, carrying clusters of galaxies with it. The force of gravity is the only counter to this expansion. Gravity is strong enough between planets and galaxies to keep them together. The gravity that stars and galaxies exert however, does not appear to be enough to stop the Universe itself expanding, and so the space between galaxies increases.

Redshift

Redshift is a term used to describe how certain galaxies in the Universe are moving away from us. We know that light travels in waves and the colour of light depends on its wavelength. When a galaxy moves away from us, light waves from it are stretched out and are red in colour – the light waves are said to be 'red-shifted'. If the galaxy is moving towards us, the light waves appear squashed together or 'blue-shifted'. Astronomers analyse a galaxy's redshift to measure the speed at which it travels. The detection of a redshift in almost all galaxies that astronomers have studied is seen by many as proof that the Universe is expanding. We cannot see redshift with the naked eye but we can detect and measure it using an instrument called a spectrograph.

REDSHIFT
This illustration shows distant galaxies red-shifting. By studying redshift, scientists have calculated that the galaxies are moving away from us at speeds of thousands of kilometres a second.

The American astronomer, Vesto Melvin Slipher, was the first to observe a redshift in a galaxy, in 1912.

EVER BIGGER
The Universe continued to expand with such energy that parts of it are still moving away from each other to this day.

GALAXIES
Some 300 million years after the Big Bang, the Universe consisted of voids surrounded by filaments of gas. Dense clumps of gas started to pull together. and, after one billion years, formed galaxies.

COSMOLOGY

Cosmology looks at the big questions about the Universe. It deals less with the make-up of individual planets and stars and more with how the Universe started, how it has evolved and how it will end – if at all.

 ## Ever-expanding Universe

No one is certain whether the Universe will last forever or will end in the distant future. Some astronomers believe that the Universe is not only expanding but will continue to do so. This is called the open Universe theory. When something has a definite beginning and end – either time or space – it is called finite. An ever-expanding universe would be infinite, it would exist over all space and for all time. However, the stars and galaxies within the Universe may slowly die leaving a vast, cold empty space.

The open Universe theory is sometimes called the Big Bore theory as there is nothing exciting to describe.

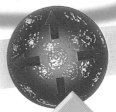
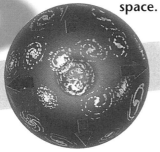
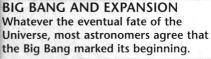

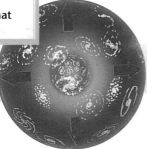

BIG BANG AND EXPANSION
Whatever the eventual fate of the Universe, most astronomers agree that the Big Bang marked its beginning.

SLOW DOWN
In the closed Universe model, there is enough mass in the Universe for gravity to slow the expansion. Eventually the expansion will be brought to a halt, and the Universe will begin to contract…

FACTS AND FIGURES

The existence of dark matter was first proposed by Swiss astronomer Fritz Zwicky in the 1930s.

Within 100,000 years of the Big Crunch, space would be hotter than our Sun. The last stars would simply boil away.

NASA's *Chandra X-ray Telescope* is used to investigate invisible areas of space, such as dark matter.

Some scientists believe the Universe's rate of expansion could be increasing.

Closed Universe

In the closed model of the Universe, scientists believe that gravity between galaxies and clusters will eventually prevent the Universe expanding any further. The galaxies may then be dragged back towards each other until they collide, forming a giant black hole. This prediction of a violent ending for the Universe is called the Big Crunch theory. Many cosmologists believe that the gravitational pull that will drag all the galaxies back together will be provided by the huge quantity of invisible matter, known as dark matter (see right) that gels the Universe together.

By the time a closed Universe slows to a halt, our own Solar System will be long dead.

Some cosmologists believe that a new Universe could emerge from the black hole created by the Big Crunch.

DATABANK

INPUT

Q How big is the Universe?

Q If the Big Crunch theory is correct, how long has the Universe got to run?

Q How much of the Universe could be made up of dark matter?

OUTPUT

A We know that the most distant galaxies from us are at least ten billion light years away.

A The Big Crunch, if it happens, will be billions of years into the future.

A As much as 90 per cent.

BIG BORE
The open Universe model has the Universe expanding forever. However, stars and galaxies will eventually grow cold and die.

RE-BIRTH
If a new Universe emerged from the Big Crunch, it could feature different laws of physics to the current Universe.

CONTRACTING
Galaxies and stars, pulled by gravity, start moving back towards each other. Space begins to heat up.

BIG CRUNCH
As the Universe contracts, black holes at the centre of galaxies merge to form one massive black hole, sucking in all matter.

Dark matter may be made up of something called WIMPS – Weakly Interacting Massive Particles.

Dark matter

One key question that perplexes cosmologists is the missing mass of the Universe. Only a small part of the Universe is visible to our eyes via optical telescopes or detected by the scientific instruments, but the gravitational pull on nearby galaxies indicates that there is invisible matter out there. It is called dark matter but no one knows what it is made of. There are plenty of ideas of what dark matter might be, including black holes, very faint stars, brown dwarfs (objects too big to be planets and too small and cold to be stars), cold gas between the stars or sub-atomic particles called neutrinos. The amount of dark matter in the Universe could have an enormous bearing on how the Universe evolved and whether it may, one day, cease to exist.

DARK QUEST
A disused coalmine in Britain is leading the search for dark matter. A detector (A) is placed 1,100m below the surface so that light and cosmic rays (blue line) will be blocked by the rock above. This will allow it to pick up dark matter (yellow lines).

MILKY WAY

The Solar System is the first line of Earth's address. The next line is the group of stars in which the Solar System is located – the galaxy known as the Milky Way. It is a fascinating place, although we have studied only a mere fraction of its stars and nebulae.

 ## First impressions

The Milky Way is a spiral galaxy with several curving arms that extend to form its disc-like shape. The Milky Way's centre is an oval shaped bulge, which is about 4,000 light years thicker than the rest of the galaxy. Although we cannot see the centre as it is shrouded in clouds of gas and dust, scientific instruments can penetrate the gloom and give us a hint of what lies inside. The centre spins faster than the rest of the galaxy and contains millions of stars, many of them red or yellow, giving the central bulge a distinctly yellowish tinge. Astronomers believe the Milky Way's centre may contain a black hole.

If the Solar System were the size of a coffee mug, the Milky Way would be the size of North America.

YOU ARE HERE
The Solar System is located within the inner edge (see arrow) of one of the Milky Way's smaller outer limbs, known as the Orion Arm. It is about 25–30,000 light years from the centre of the galaxy.

SLIVER OF SPACE
This infrared image removes intervening dust and gas to show that the Milky Way, when viewed edge on, is a thin disc.

 ## Features of the Milky Way

Although the view of much of the Milky Way is obstructed, astronomers have identified many different features including a large number of nebulae. The illustration at the bottom left of this page shows some of the Sun's neighbours in the galaxy. These are: 1. Cone Nebula; 2. Rosette Nebula; 3. Orion Nebula; 4. Lagoon Nebula; 5. Our Solar System; 6. California Nebula; 7. Trifid Nebula; 8. Vela Supernova Remnant; 9. North America Nebula. Each of these nebulae is in the process of creating new stars.

A galactic year is the time it takes the Solar System to orbit the Milky Way's centre.

BITE OF MILKY WAY
While some galaxies appear to have no nebulae and therefore no potential for new stars, the Milky Way has many.

Birth of the Milky Way

FACTS AND FIGURES

Even at a speed of 240 km per second the Sun takes 220 million years to orbit the centre of the Milky Way.

Although a relatively small galaxy, the Milky Way has a mass equal to about 1,000 billion Suns.

Light takes 12 hours to cross the Solar System but takes 100,000 years to cross the Milky Way.

The nearest galaxy to the Milky Way, the Sagittarius galaxy, is being ripped apart by the Milky Way's gravity.

Gravity is pulling the Milky Way and Andromeda galaxies together at a speed of 300 km per second.

The total mass of all the stars in the Milky Way is equal to about 200 million of our Suns.

The Milky Way formed some five billion years after the Big Bang. A massive cloud of hydrogen and helium gas started to collapse in on itself under the influence of gravity. The gas at the centre was pulled tightly together until it was dense enough to begin forming stars. This proto-galaxy started spinning and, as its speed increased, the outer area flattened out into a disc shape. Gradually, key features of the Milky Way formed, such as its wispy, tendril-like arms. Scientists studying the birth of other galaxies believe that those that spin slowly during formation become irregular or elliptical galaxies.

The word galaxy comes from the Greek word for milk. Ancient Greeks believed the Milky Way was milk from the gods.

SPINNING CLOUD
A slowly-spinning mass of gas collapses and draws matter towards its centre to form stars. It starts to spin faster.

A SHAPE EMERGES
Gas clouds merge within the swirling disc, and the force of gravity attracts more material. Arms begin to take shape.

FRESH GALAXY
The galaxy is now fully formed. The arms contain many nebulae, and continue to produce new stars.

MILLIONS OF MILKY WAYS
This photograph shows just a tiny portion of space. Even so, it is clear that there are countless other galaxies out there.

The Magellanic Clouds are small irregular galaxies that orbit the Milky Way once every 1.5 billion years.

DATABANK

INPUT	OUTPUT
Q How many stars are there in the Milky Way?	**A** Around 200 billion.
Q How did the Milky Way get its spiral shape?	**A** It became flattened into a disc shape by its spinning round.
Q When did we discover that the Milky Way was a spiral galaxy?	**A** American astronomer, William Morgan proved this in 1951.
Q Do we know where the exact centre of the Milky Way is?	**A** Yes. Astronomers place it in an area called Sagittarius A.

GALAXIES

How many galaxies does the Universe contain? Ten thousand? Half a million? Astronomers estimate that a staggering 100 billion galaxies in numerous shapes and sizes exist across space, gathered into clusters.

 ## Galaxy types

In 1924, Edwin Hubble proved that other galaxies existed beyond the Milky Way. Astronomers catalogue galaxies in several ways but the most important factor is their basic shape. More than half of all galaxies observed are elliptical which means round or oval in shape. The other common shapes are spiral galaxies, like the Milky Way, and barred spirals which have a central bar of material running through centre. A fourth type, called irregular galaxies, include those that don't fit into any of the above classes. Irregular galaxies tend to have no obvious shape and are rich in gas and dust. Spiral and barred spirals galaxies are further classified into four groups according to how large their centres are, and how tight their arms wind round the centre. Elliptical galaxies are divided into eight different classes from E0 to E7. E0 galaxies are almost ball-shaped while E7 galaxies resemble flattened ovals.

SPIRAL AND BARRED SPIRAL
Spiral galaxies (left) have loosely or tightly wound arms. Barred spiral galaxies (above) have a central bar between the spirals.

Elliptical galaxies seem to have no nebulae, which means they cannot form new stars.

ELLIPTICAL AND IRREGULAR
Elliptical galaxies (above) range in shape from ovals to spheres. Irregular galaxies (right) have no recognizable shape.

 ## Active galaxies

A small number of galaxies have very luminous cores, which pump energy and material into space. These are known as active galaxies and come in a range of types, including radio galaxies, quasars and Seyfert galaxies. Quasars are among the most powerful objects in the Universe and also the most distant from Earth. Astronomers believe that a huge black hole lies at an active galaxy's centre. As the gas and, possibly, complete stars are sucked into the black hole, huge amounts of energy in the form of radio waves, infrared, light and x-rays are sent into space. Earth's nearest quasar is PKS 2349-01, 1.5 million light years away.

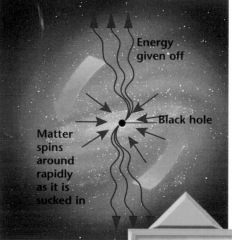

Energy given off

Black hole

Matter spins around rapidly as it is sucked in

QUASAR
A quasar may contain a black hole. As it draws in matter, the black hole ejects vast amounts of energy.

FACTS AND FIGURES

Malin 1 is the largest galaxy recorded. It is thought to be 1,000 times more massive than the Milky Way.

Dwarf elliptical galaxies are believed to be the most common type of galaxy in the entire Universe.

The first-ever quasar to be discovered was by the Dutch astronomer, Maarten Schmidt in 1963.

Irregular galaxies are thought to have been pulled out of shape by the gravity of other nearby galaxies.

Virgo III cloud

Virgo II cloud

Virgo I cloud

Local Group (Canes Venatici cloud)

Leo II cloud

Crater cloud

LOCAL GROUP
Our Local Group can be shown as a sphere five million light years across. This image names some of its main galaxies.

Leo A

Triangulum (M33)

Andromeda

GR8

Milky Way

Pisces

NGC 6822

Galaxy clusters

Galaxies exist in larger groups called clusters, held together by the pull of gravity. Our own galaxy, the Milky Way, is the second largest of at least 30 galaxies that form a cluster called the Local Group (right), which can be pictured as a sphere 5 million light years wide. The Local Group, contains a range of fascinating galaxies, such as Andromeda (the largest), Triangulam (the third largest) and smaller Pisces. The galaxy Leo A is the most distant member of the group. The most common types of galaxy in the group are the 15 or so dwarf galaxies.

The Andromeda galaxy in our Local Group is the most distant object visible to the naked eye.

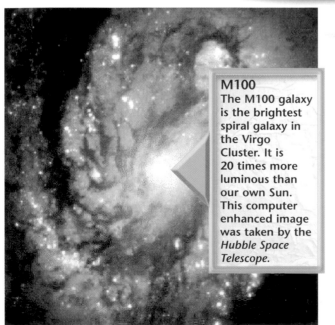

M100
The M100 galaxy is the brightest spiral galaxy in the Virgo Cluster. It is 20 times more luminous than our own Sun. This computer enhanced image was taken by the *Hubble Space Telescope*.

Supercluster

Although huge, our Local Group is an outlying and minor part of a massive collection of galaxies known as the Coma-Virgo Supercluster (see top). As well as our Local Group of galaxies, the supercluster holds ten other clouds of galaxies. The supercluster measures around 100 million light years across. At its centre lies the Virgo Cluster. The supercluster is a fascinating grouping of more than 2,000 galaxies over 50 million light years away. It is often referred to as a galactic zoo as it contains examples of all the major galaxy types. Its proximity to Earth and bright, well-spaced galaxies makes it relatively easy to observe.

The Virgo cluster's M87 galaxy ejects a continuous jet of gassy material 5,000 light years in length.

EARLY SKYWATCHING

Skywatching is not new. From images and positions of stars painted onto cave walls 10,000 years ago, we know that people have always been fascinated with the skies.

 ## Ancient skywatchers

Many ancient civilisations studied the night sky – from the Babylonians, Egyptians and Polynesians to cultures in central and South America. Archaeologists have unearthed a number of artifacts that show star maps and record the position of the Sun, Moon and Earth.

> In Chinese tradition, astronomers Hsi and Ho were executed in 2137BC when they failed to predict an eclipse.

Early skywatchers also observed comets with sparkling tails, and meteors or shooting stars apparently falling from the sky. All over the world, ancient astronomers observed points of light that appeared to move among the stars. They called these objects planets, meaning wanderers. Their present names are taken from those of the Roman gods – Jupiter, the king of the gods; Mars, the god of war; Mercury, the messenger of the gods, Venus, the goddess of love and beauty; and Saturn, the god of agriculture.

HEAVENS ABOVE
The ancient Egyptians studied the Sun, Moon and stars and based many of their festivals on the movement of these bodies.

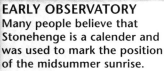

EARLY OBSERVATORY
Many people believe that Stonehenge is a calender and was used to mark the position of the midsummer sunrise.

DATABANK

Q What is the Dresden Codex?

A It is an Ancient Mayan text from South America showing details of the Moon and Venus.

Q Who was the first woman to be connected with astronomy?

A Hyspatria of Alexandria taught astronomy and mathematics 1,600 years ago.

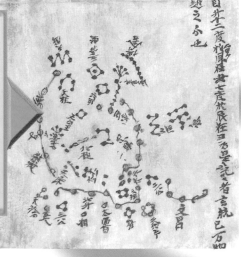

STAR MAP
Many remnants of Chinese star maps have been found. They show parts of the night sky mapped in superb detail. This map features the constellation we call the Plough or Great Bear.

 ## Chinese stargazers

In many early cultures, the study and knowledge of the stars was heavily bound up in religion. The incredible sights in the night sky were believed to be gods or spirits in action. The Chinese have a long history of recording astronomical phenomena. In the past they believed that earthly events were influenced by what happened in the heavens. Historians have found records of eclipses from the second millenn... BC and, about 2,400 years ago, the Chinese astronomer... -shen catalogued 809 stars.

Ancient Greeks

The Ancient Greeks took astronomy very seriously, turning it into a science. Hipparchus and Ptolemy were among the most important Greek astronomers. Hipparchus constructed the first in-depth star chart in which he named around 850 stars. He also predicted the positions of the planets and attempted to estimate the distance of the Moon from Earth. The astronomer and geographer Ptolemy is most famous for his theory that the Earth was the centre of the entire Universe. The Ptolemaic view portrayed all the planets as well as the Sun and Moon revolving around the Earth with the night sky made up of a giant sphere of never-changing stars, which also revolved around Earth. His views were accepted until the 16th and 17th centuries.

PTOLEMY
Ptolemy (AD85–165) lived in Alexandria in Egypt during the time of Roman occupation. His ideas were taken up by the Byzantines – the successors to the Roman Empire – and later the Arabs.

SELF-CENTRED
Ptolemy's view of an Earth-centred Universe was based on the ideas of earlier great scientists such as Aristotle and Plato.

Saturn

Venus

Earth

Mercury

Jupiter

Moon

Sun

Mars

Saturn

Jupiter

Venus

Mercury

Sun

Earth

DANGEROUS IDEA?
Many people thought that Copernicus' idea of a Sun-centred Universe directly challenged the Bible.

Moon

Mars

FACTS AND FIGURES

The Dogon tribe of West Africa knew of Saturn's rings thousands of years before their existence was confirmed.

Ptolemy's famous book, the *Almagest* is a collection of 13 books, which were translated by Arab scholars into one.

Over a hundred stars still carry the names originally given to them many centuries ago.

Native North Americans used sighting the Pleiades group of stars as a way of testing a warrior's eyesight.

Tycho Brahe lost most of his nose in a duel. He wore a false silver, gold and wax nose for the rest of his life.

The Copernican Revolution

Ptolemy's view of Earth as centre of the Universe held sway for 1,500 years. It was first challenged by a Polish monk and astronomer, Nikolas Copernicus. His theory, which placed the Sun at the centre of the Universe, has been proven wrong but he was correct that the planets orbit the Sun. Copernicus' views clashed with the church, which believed in Ptolemy's model. It took the work of astronomers like Tycho Brahe, Johannes Kepler and Galileo before Copernicus' view of the Solar System was accepted.

MULTI-TA[...]
Coperni[...]
only a[...]
[...]ok,
[...]ax
[...]r and physician.

In the 1600s, Danish astronomer Tycho Brahe calculated the length of an Earth year to within one second.

STARGAZING

From Earth, the night sky appears to be a filled with a confusing array of stars. Groups of stars, called constellations act as a sort of road map and help us navigate through the heavens.

NIGHT VISION
It takes about 30 minutes for our eyes to become accustomed to the night sky so that we can see objects more clearly.

The sky at night

Beginners often find skywatching confusing at first because the stars appear to move each night. Although stars seem to keep their positions relative to each other, they appear in a slightly different place each evening, and gently 'drift' across the sky during the night. This movement is largely caused by Earth's passage around the Sun. One tricky obstacle for the astronomer is light pollution. This is caused by city lights, which spread their glow across parts of the night sky drowning out fainter stars. On a clear night, stranger sights may be found among the stars, planets and galaxies on show. Meteor showers and comets sometimes appear, while people living near the north or south poles may be treated to an aurora. These wonderful light shows occur as particles from the Sun are attracted to Earth's magnetic poles.

Inexperienced skywatchers commonly report Venus as an Unidentified Flying Object (UFO).

Celestial sphere

Originally a constellation was regarded as a star system but now it refers to an area of the sky. The idea of constellations can be confusing so astronomers refer to the celestial sphere – an imaginary sphere surrounding Earth with the stars all inside. The constellations are dotted around the sphere's surface, which is usually divided into a grid to allow stargazers to locate easily a particular area.

The stars within a constellation may not belong to the same galaxy or even the same galaxy cluster.

SKY MAP
The celestial sphere is an imaginary globe surrounding Earth with its north and south poles aligned with those of Earth. It is a convenient way to map three dimensional space from Earth.

Different skies

The celestial sphere is divided into two halves known as hemispheres (see below). People living in the northern hemisphere can only see northern constellations and a few stars from the south, while people in the south see the opposite. Additionally, Earth's orbit and rotation mean that only a few of each hemisphere's constellations can be seen at any one time.

The International Astronomical Union decides the names of constellations and new stars and galaxies.

Pegasus

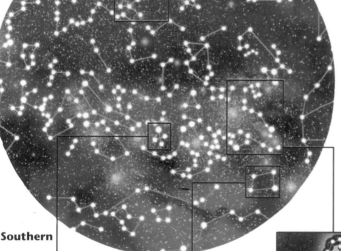

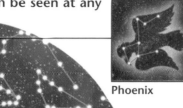

Phoenix

Northern

Southern

Crux (Southern Cross)

Libra

Scorpio

Hercules

Ursa Major

Leo

Astrologers believe that the movement of planets within the zodiac has a strong influence on human affairs.

DATABANK

Q What is a planisphere?

A It is a circular map of the stars showing where they will be on a certain day or at a certain time.

Q Who discovered the first constellations?

A The Babylonians are believed to have found the first constellations before 2000BC.

 # The zodiac

One band of 12 constellations runs right round the celestial sphere. Known as the zodiac, these constellations feature the names of the star signs used in astrology. The Moon, Sun and all of the planets except Pluto travel across the sky within this band of stars. The Sun appears to spend roughly a month in each constellation of the zodiac.

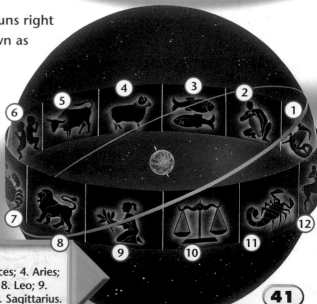

SIGNS OF THE ZODIAC
1. Capricorn; 2. Aquarius; 3. Pisces; 4. Aries; 5. Taurus; 6. Gemini; 7. Cancer; 8. Leo; 9. Virgo; 10. Libra; 11. Scorpio; 12. Sagittarius.

TELESCOPES

Until the 17th century, people relied on the naked eye to view the skies. The invention of optical telescopes has enabled astronomers to peer into the far reaches of space.

 ## Refracting telescopes

Dutch optics makers exhibited the first telescopes in 1608. They placed two spectacle lenses in a tube and found that distant objects appeared closer than before. The lenses bent, or refracted, the light and enlarged the image. Italian astronomer Galileo quickly latched onto the new invention, and built a telescope with 30 times the magnification of the human eye. He used it to study the night sky. However, larger lenses are difficult to build. Above 1m in diameter, it is almost impossible for a lens to support its own weight.

EARLY TELESCOPE
Early refracting telescopes were very long in order to give the viewer a clear image of the stars.

Large lenses can suffer from chromatic aberration – coloured fringing that appears around an image.

The world's largest refracting telescope is at Yerkes Observatory, Wisconsin, USA. Built in 1897, its aperture is 1.06m.

Refracting telescope
Light rays
Eyepiece
Object lens

TELESCOPES
While refractors use lenses to enlarge images, reflectors rely on curved mirrors to magnify light waves.

Reflecting telescope
Object mirror
Curved mirror
Light rays
Eyepiece

 ## Reflecting telescopes

To see further and in more detail, bigger telescopes were required with more light-gathering power than refracting telescopes. Reflecting telescopes, first introduced in 1668, now comprise all of the world's largest telescopes.

These use large, ultra-smooth mirrors – easier to build than large lenses – to collect light. Our eyes have an opening, or aperture, of up to 7mm to let light in. Reflecting telescopes can have apertures measured in metres. Reflecting telescopes send their images to computers and scientific instruments, which split the light up into different wavelengths, or to a charge-coupled device – a powerful, high resolution form of digital camera.

HOME-MADE
William Herschel (1738–1822) built a large reflecting telescope in his garden in Britain. The opening or aperture was 1.2m wide, and the viewer stood on a platform below this in order to study very faint objects.

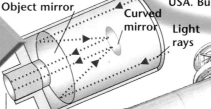

LOOKING UP
This astronomical telescope, sited on Mount Palomar in California has a reflector over 5m in diameter. Called the *200 Inch Hale*, it was the world's largest reflecting telescope from 1947 until 1970.

In 1838, telescopes allowed astronomers to measure the distance from Earth to a star for the first time.

Hubble

Telescopes placed in orbit around Earth overcome the obstacle of Earth's thick atmosphere and allow uninterrupted viewing of the Universe beyond our Solar System. The *Hubble Space Telescope* is the most famous example. Orbiting at 610km above Earth's surface, *Hubble* has made vital discoveries that have changed what we know about space. In 1995, for example, *Hubble* photographed star birth in the Eagle Nebula, and produced a view of galaxies up to 10 billion light years away. *Hubble's* solar panels generate the electricity to power its reflecting telescope and other instruments that allow it to see infrared and ultraviolet waves being emitted from distant stars and galaxies.

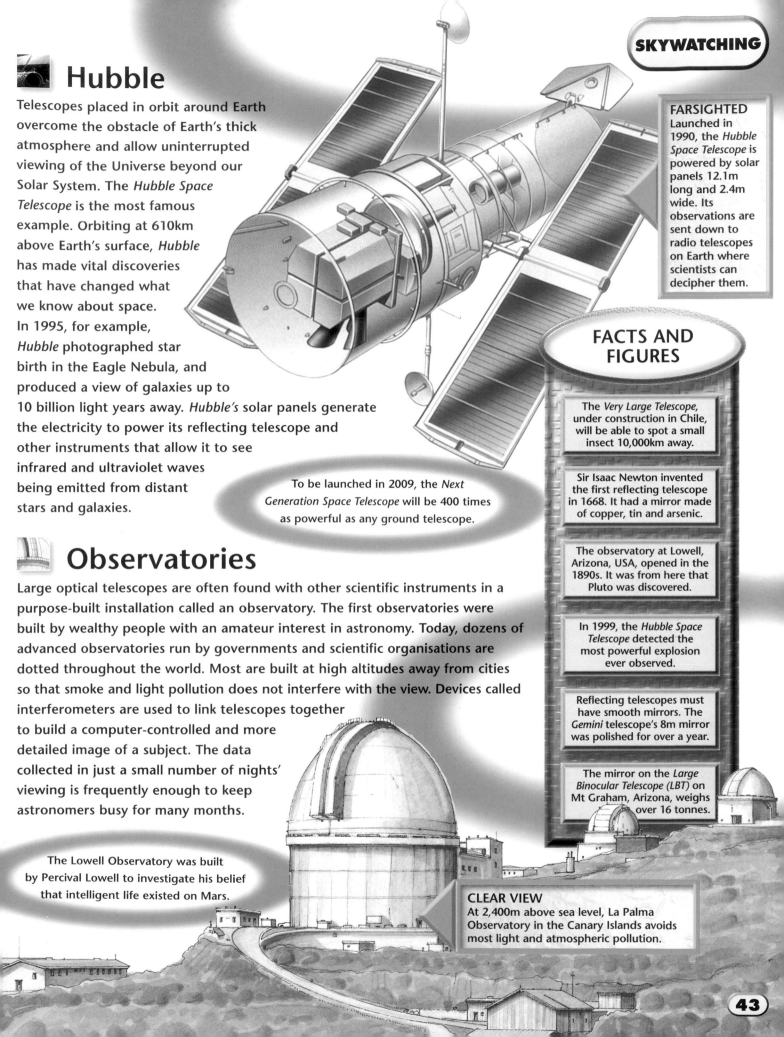

FARSIGHTED
Launched in 1990, the *Hubble Space Telescope* is powered by solar panels 12.1m long and 2.4m wide. Its observations are sent down to radio telescopes on Earth where scientists can decipher them.

To be launched in 2009, the *Next Generation Space Telescope* will be 400 times as powerful as any ground telescope.

FACTS AND FIGURES

The *Very Large Telescope*, under construction in Chile, will be able to spot a small insect 10,000km away.

Sir Isaac Newton invented the first reflecting telescope in 1668. It had a mirror made of copper, tin and arsenic.

The observatory at Lowell, Arizona, USA, opened in the 1890s. It was from here that Pluto was discovered.

In 1999, the *Hubble Space Telescope* detected the most powerful explosion ever observed.

Reflecting telescopes must have smooth mirrors. The *Gemini* telescope's 8m mirror was polished for over a year.

The mirror on the *Large Binocular Telescope (LBT)* on Mt Graham, Arizona, weighs over 16 tonnes.

Observatories

Large optical telescopes are often found with other scientific instruments in a purpose-built installation called an observatory. The first observatories were built by wealthy people with an amateur interest in astronomy. Today, dozens of advanced observatories run by governments and scientific organisations are dotted throughout the world. Most are built at high altitudes away from cities so that smoke and light pollution does not interfere with the view. Devices called interferometers are used to link telescopes together to build a computer-controlled and more detailed image of a subject. The data collected in just a small number of nights' viewing is frequently enough to keep astronomers busy for many months.

The Lowell Observatory was built by Percival Lowell to investigate his belief that intelligent life existed on Mars.

CLEAR VIEW
At 2,400m above sea level, La Palma Observatory in the Canary Islands avoids most light and atmospheric pollution.

NON-OPTICAL TELESCOPES

Scientists have learned that visible light is just one of several types of electromagnetic radiation that reach us from space. Radio telescopes and other instruments have been developed to collect information from these sources and peer far beyond the visible Universe.

 ## Radio telescopes

As well as sending out light waves, many objects in space emit radio waves, which are invisible to the human eye or optical telescopes. We have learned how to collect these radio waves in order to detect and learn about objects too distant or not bright enough to be seen with optical telescopes. Most radio telescopes (see left) use a concave (curved inwards or bowl-shaped) dish to collect radio waves from space. The radio waves are reflected from the dish to an antenna, which sends the signal to an amplifier in the receiver where the signal is amplified (strengthened). Computers are used to process the signal into images and data, which can be analysed by radio astronomers.

Reflector dish

Antenna

Tilt

Receiver

Revolving base

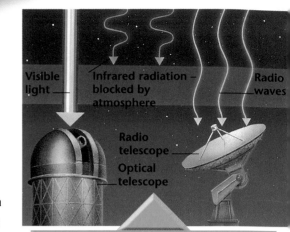

Visible light

Infrared radiation – blocked by atmosphere

Radio waves

Radio telescope

Optical telescope

OPTICAL VERSES RADIO
Radio waves and visible light waves pass through Earth's atmosphere and are picked up by optical and radio telescopes.

RADIO TELESCOPE
Radio telescopes can be moved to follow a particular celestial body's progress across the sky or to view different parts of space.

Amateur US astronomer, Grote Reber, built one of the first radio telescopes. It was made partly from bits of a car.

 ## Single dishes and arrays

Unlike optical telescopes, radio telescopes operate 24 hours a day and can still work through thick cloud and air pollution. However, radio waves have less energy than light waves. There are two solutions to this obstacle: build very large dishes to collect enough detail or link many smaller dishes together to form what is called an array. Examples of both single dishes and arrays may be found throughout the world.

WORLD'S LARGEST ARRAY
The *Very Large Array (VLA)* telescope in the USA, has 27 dishes. It simulates the effect of a single dish 27km wide.

The data from the dishes of the *Very Large Array* are combined to produce one radio image.

Infrared astronomy

Infrared waves lie just beyond the visible spectrum of light. Everything in the Universe cooler than around 3,000°C emits some infrared radiation. Infrared telescopes on Earth and in space are used to look at the cooler elements of the Universe and can detect objects as cold as dust clouds at -200°C. Infrared astronomy has revealed thousands of galaxies never observed before, and has discovered water vapour in space.

DEEPER VISION
NASA's *Infrared Telescope Facility (IRTF)* in Hawaii is used to study planet atmospheres and dust clouds in space.

JUPITER REVEALED
The red and yellow bands in this infrared image of Jupiter show the hottest areas of the planet's surface.

DATABANK

Q Who was the first person to detect radio waves from space?

A American Karl Jansky discovered radio waves from space in 1932.

Q What features have radio telescopes discovered about the Universe?

A The many finds include quasars, pulsars and background radiation from the Big Bang.

FACTS AND FIGURES

The world's first professional radio telescope was built at Jodrell Bank, Cheshire, England in 1947.

Infrared telescopes detected 3,000km-long plumes when comet Shoemaker-Levy 9 hit Jupiter in 1994.

An ultraviolet observatory was set up on the Moon in 1972 by the crew of the *Apollo 16* lunar mission.

The largest radio telescope dish in the world is the *Arecibo* dish in Puerto Rico. It is 305m in diameter.

The first ultraviolet telescope in space was the *Copernicus Satellite Telescope*, launched in 1972.

Gamma rays are high energy waves created by radioactive decay and by nuclear reactions in stars.

Checking out other waves

Radio, light and infrared waves are not the only types of signal we receive from space. Astronomers are also using scientific instruments to detect and measure x-rays and gamma rays in space. To track down the hottest stars in the Universe, those with temperatures above 10,000°C, astronomers are turning to ultraviolet telescopes and instruments. Most ultraviolet telescopes are fitted to orbiting satellites because ultraviolet light reaching Earth from space is largely absorbed by Earth's atmosphere and does not reach the ground.

RADAR IMAGING
An image of a planet's surface can be built up by beaming radio waves at the planet and then interpreting the returning echo.

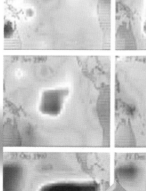

MICROWAVES
Taken by the *Microwave Limb Sounder* satellite, these images show the movement of water vapour over the Pacific Ocean.

BLAST-OFF

Gravity keeps us on Earth. To escape its strong pull and head out into space, rockets must travel incredibly fast – over 11 km per second! This speed is known as 'escape velocity'.

WAR – THE MOTHER OF INVENTION
Space rockets evolved from rocket missiles like this German V2, a number of which attacked Britain during World War II.

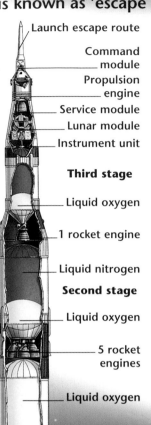

- Launch escape route
- Command module
- Propulsion engine
- Service module
- Lunar module
- Instrument unit
- **Third stage**
- Liquid oxygen
- 1 rocket engine
- Liquid nitrogen
- **Second stage**
- Liquid oxygen
- 5 rocket engines
- Liquid oxygen
- **First stage**
- Kerosene fuel

 ## Rocket pioneers

The Chinese fired simple firework-style rockets over 800 years ago, but it wasn't until the 20th century that rockets were used to send objects into space. The Russian scientist Konstantin Tsiolovsky (1857–1935) was the first to seriously suggest the idea. Development work was performed by many scientists and engineers including Herman Oberth, Robert H. Goddard and Wernher von Braun. In 1926, Goddard, a US scientist, became the first to launch a small rocket propelled by liquid fuel. Oberth and von Braun were both Germans who, after World War II, worked on rockets for the American space programme, including the Saturn 5 rocket.

Although rockets send humans and probes into space, they are most commonly used to launch commercial satellites.

 ## Multi-stage rockets

Single-stage rockets can reach low Earth orbit but they don't have the power to break completely free of Earth's gravity. The solution has been to build rockets that work in stages. As one stage uses up its fuel and therefore power, it separates from the rest of the rocket and falls away. This reduces the weight being carried and allows rockets to carry craft out of low Earth orbit and into space. The Russian Vostok launcher had two stages and launched the first ever satellite into space, *Sputnik 1*, and the first person in space, Yuri Gagarin. These were just two of its 150 missions.

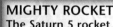

MIGHTY ROCKET
The Saturn 5 rocket, which was used on the manned Moon missions, consisted of three stages, each with its own fuel tank.

FIRST STAGE
As the Saturn 5 rocket leaves Earth's atmosphere, the first stage falls away to be burned up in the outer atmosphere.

SECOND STAGE
This fires for six minutes pushing the rocket to 22,000 km/h. It is finally jettisoned 190km above Earth.

Re-usable rockets

Rockets are single-use objects, which makes space missions incredibly expensive. Throughout the 1970s, space agencies worked on designs for re-usable space launchers that would take off like a rocket but glide back to Earth like an airplane. NASA's space shuttle was the result. It consists of an orbiter craft, two solid fuel rocket boosters and a giant external fuel tank 47m long and 8.4m in diameter. At take-off, the shuttle's engines and two booster rockets provide power equal to that of over 130 jumbo jets. The boosters are emptied and fall away just two minutes into the launch. They are usually recovered and can be used again. The external tank is jettisoned later and burns up in Earth's atmosphere. After completing its mission, the shuttle re-enters the atmosphere and glides down to land on an extra-long runway.

Future spacecraft aim to re-use even more material in the hope of saving up to 90 per cent of the cost of a mission.

FACTS AND FIGURES

From 1960–1990 the Delta rocket made 200 launches, making it one of the world's longest serving rockets.

The Russian Soyuz family of rocket launchers have performed over 1,630 successful missions.

The European Space Agency craft *Ulysses* made the fastest ever escape velocity. It reached 54,614 km/h.

The crew of *Apollo 10*, reached 39,897 km/h, the fastest speed humans have ever travelled.

It takes at least 55 days to prepare a shuttle for launch. During take-off, the craft uses 242,240 litres of fuel a minute.

There are over 32,000 heat-resistant tiles covering the shuttle. These protect it as it re-enters Earth's atmosphere.

BOOSTERS
Just two minutes after lift-off, the pair of solid fuel boosters are exhausted. They fall away from the shuttle and parachutes open to cushion their descent into the ocean. They can be re-used up to 20 times.

The Soviet Union (now The Russian Federation) built and tested its own space shuttle in the 1980s.

THIRD STAGE
The third stage fires twice before releasing the Apollo spacecraft and lunar modules towards the Moon.

DATABANK

INPUT	OUTPUT
Q Apart from the USA, who else launches their own rockets?	**A** The European Space Agency, Russia, India, Japan and China.
Q When was the first shuttle launched and what was its name?	**A** The first shuttle into space was *Columbia*, in 1981.
Q How many space shuttles have been built by NASA?	**A** Six – *Columbia, Atlantis, Challenger, Discovery, Endeavour & Enterprise*.

ARTIFICIAL SATELLITES

Objects sent into orbit are called satellites. Since 1957, over 4,000 satellites have been launched. They perform tasks such as forecasting weather and relaying telephone and TV transmissions all over the world.

Orbiting Earth

All satellites are designed to obtain information of some kind and communicate it back to ground stations on Earth via radio transmitters. Satellites are launched by rocket or carried into space by the shuttle. Once in orbit, satellites must travel at a precise speed that keeps them at a consistent distance from Earth at all times. This prevents the craft from falling back into the atmosphere and being destroyed.

Some satellites have tiny jet thrusters on board that make small changes to the satellite's position to keep it on the correct path.

Some satellites are launched directly from the cargo bay of the space shuttle.

SUN DRIVEN
Most satellites are powered by batteries charged by solar cells in the wing panels or wrapped around the satellite's body.

DATABANK

Q How many countries have their own satellites?

A Just over 35, including Sweden, Chile, Egypt and Thailand. The UK currently has 17 in orbit.

Q Do spy satellites exist?

A Yes. From their orbits hundreds of kilometres above Earth they can detect objects 10cm wide.

Triggering the space race

Competition between the USA and the former Soviet Union led to the space race. The Russians scored first by launching the first successful artificial satellite, *Sputnik 1,* in October 1957. *Sputnik 1* was a metal ball 58cm across that orbited the Earth once every 96 minutes, sending back radio signals. After 92 days it burnt up in the Earth's atmosphere. Four months after *Sputnik's* launch, the US launched their first satellite, *Explorer 1.* It detected belts of radiation around the Earth, later named the Van Allen belts.

SIMPLE SATELLITE
Launched by the Russian A1 rocket, *Sputnik 1* weighed 83.6kg. It transmitted radio signals from its four antennae.

Geostationary satellites

A satellite in a geostationary orbit – approximately 36,000km above Earth – circles our planet once every 24 hours, the same amount of time it takes the Earth to spin on its axis. This means that it stays above the same part of Earth's surface all the time. At such a distance, the satellite can examine a vast portion of Earth's surface – this viewing area is called the satellite's footprint. Geostationary satellites are used to transmit thousands of global telephone calls and television signals every second.

Watching Earth

Many satellites are designed to watch Earth in some way. Since the launch of the first weather satellite, *Tiros 1*, in 1960, weather or meteorological satellites have continually monitored weather patterns and climate conditions as well as helped forecast potentially dangerous weather systems, such as hurricanes. In the past, such disasters would strike with little warning. Satellites can also map the locations of minerals, water, and types of vegetation. As well as providing clues to where to find new resources, they help us understand how well or poorly people are managing Earth's ecology. For example, the satellite *Nimbus 7* discovered a hole in Earth's ozone layer.

> Science fiction writer Arthur C. Clarke predicted the development of satellites long before they were invented.

DIFFERENT ORBITS
As well as the geostationary orbit (above) there is also low Earth orbit, elliptical or Molniya orbit and polar orbit.

FACTS AND FIGURES

Between 900 and 1,000 new commercial satellites are due to be launched by the year 2008.

In 1984, *Solar Max*, launched in 1980, became the first satellite to be repaired in space by the space shuttle.

NASA estimates that there are 9,000 man-made objects orbiting Earth. Many of these are debris from rockets.

The largest satellite in orbit is the *Galaxy 11*. It weighs 4.5 tonnes and has a wingspan of 31m.

Intelsat's *Early Bird* satellite, launched in 1965, was the world's very first communications satellite.

WEATHER EYE
Weather satellites play a vital role in forecasting and following existing weather patterns. Hanging in geostationary orbits, such satellites monitor wind speed, clouds, sea temperature and other conditions.

MAPPING
The *Landsat 4* satellite maps the Earth. It can detect pollution or analyse rocks and minerals. It can even find oil.

SHUTTLE
Even the space shuttle carries remote sensing instruments for scanning and mapping Earth in detail.

EARLY SPACE MISSIONS

On April 12, 1961, in a mission lasting just one hour and 48 minutes, Russian cosmonaut Yuri Gagarin orbited the Earth inside a tiny spacecraft, *Vostok 1*. His pioneering journey has led the way for hundreds more missions carrying people into space.

Fuel rockets jettisoned

Take off

CM re-enters atmosphere

Splash down

Pioneer missions

The race into space saw both the Soviet Union and the USA accelerate their space programmes. After the Soviets scored a collection of notable firsts including the first man in space, the first woman in space and the first spacewalk, attention shifted to getting a person onto the Moon. Just seven years after Gagarin's historic journey, the USA's *Apollo 8* became the first manned space vehicle to orbit the Moon. Five months later, *Apollo 10* came to within 15km of the Moon's surface to act as a dress rehearsal for a full-scale moon landing.

RUSSIANS IN SPACE
Yuri Gagarin's *Vostok 1* was the first of six Vostok craft. Later Russian manned spacecraft included Voskhod and Soyuz.

In 1975 a Russian and a US craft docked in space. The crews shook hands to symbolise future co-operation.

Life aboard a spacecraft

Conditions aboard early spacecraft were uncomfortable. Food was barely palatable and crew members were forced to wear bulky spacesuits at all times because the cabins were unpressurised. Tragically, in 1971 the crew of the Russian *Soyuz 11* died when their cabin depressurised. In space all astronauts encounter a lack of gravity known as weightlessness. This makes tasks such as eating, sleeping and working much more difficult than on Earth. Early missions allowed scientists to develop basic showers, cooking equipment and toilets to cope with weightlessness. The facilities aboard the space shuttle and space stations are far more sophisticated.

JUNK FOOD
The first space food was nutritious but unappetising dried cubes and liquid mush. It has improved since!

If not kept under control, liquid turns into a floating spherical blob in weightless conditions.

CAREFUL
Weightlessness means that going to the toilet in space is a delicate operation. Hand holds and foot restraints keep the astronaut in place. A vacuum maintains a seal between the astronaut and the seat.

TO THE MOON (RED)
After the main fuel sections of the rocket are jettisoned, the Command and Service Module (CSM) heads for the Moon.

Rocket heads to Moon

LM blasts off and rejoins CSM

Command Module (CM) detaches

CSM turns around and docks with Lunar Module (LM)

Crew enter LM and land

HOME TO EARTH (PINK)
Part of the Lunar Module takes off from the Moon and rejoins the Command and Service Module before heading to Earth.

To the Moon

The most famous manned space mission is the first Apollo Moon landing. On July 16, 1969, the massive Saturn V rocket launched the *Apollo 11* mission into space. In a complicated set of manoeuvres, the Command and Service Module (CSM) containing astronaut, Michael Collins, orbited the Moon whilst the Lunar Module, holding astronauts Neil Armstrong and Buzz Aldrin, descended to the Moon's surface and landed late on July 20, 1969. Watched by over 600 million people on television, Armstrong and Aldrin stepped out onto the Moon's surface the following morning, planted an American flag and collected 21.7kg of rock and dust samples. Once back inside the Lunar Module, they blasted off and docked with the CSM, which then returned to Earth. The Command Module, with the astronauts on board detached itself from the Service Module and splashed down in the Pacific Ocean on the 24th July. Six more Apollo missions were to follow.

MAKING HISTORY
Filmed by a camera mounted on the Lunar Module *Eagle*, Neil Armstrong stepped tentatively out onto the Moon's surface.

SPLIT PERSONALITY
The Lunar Module was a two-part craft. The crew blasted off from the Moon in the top section leaving the bottom half behind.

The longest time anyone has spent on the Moon is 74 hours 59 minutes, during the *Apollo 17* mission.

SPLASH DOWN
NASA's astronauts use parachutes to land their astronauts in the sea. Russia's cosmonauts usually come down on land.

DATABANK

Q Who was the first woman in space and what nationality was she?

A The Russian Valentina Tereshkova orbited Earth in 1963. She was 26 years old.

Q Who performed the first walk in space and when did it happen?

A In 1965, Soviet cosmonaut Alexei Leonov made the first space walk.

SPACE SHUTTLE

Since the pioneering visits to the Moon, the American space programme has been concentrated around the space shuttle. Versatile and re-usable, the space shuttle has performed a variety of fascinating and daring tasks, from repairing broken satellites to ferrying astronauts to and from space stations.

Working inside and out

Astronauts' work on early missions was usually confined to reporting back to Earth on their own condition and that of their craft. Today, they have a wider range of tasks to perform, in missions that last up to a week. Many experiments – from growing crystals in space to testing new equipment – are undertaken inside the shuttle. Satellites and other space hardware are deployed from the shuttle's large cargo bay. This may involve the use of the Remote Manipulator System (RMS). This robot arm is controlled from inside the shuttle and can move huge amounts of cargo. Crew members don EVA space suits (see page 55) in order to perform missions outside the craft.

FLIGHT DECK
The space shuttle pilot and the payload commander monitor a space walk from the flight deck.

CABIN
The shuttle and the robot arm are operated from the flight deck. Below this are the crew's quarters.

Capture and repair

Some of the most vital work that space shuttle crews have engaged in has been correcting problems with probes, satellites and telescopes already in space but not working properly. A repair mission must first capture the object orbiting in space using a delicate set of manoeuvres often involving the RMS robot arm and astronauts in EVA suits (see page 55). Once the item is safely under control, it can be repaired before being released to perform its mission. In 1992, the STS-49 shuttle mission was extended by two days to capture the *Intelsat 6* satellite, which had been in an unusable orbit since its launch. Crew members fitted a live rocket motor to the satellite, which successfully propelled it into its correct orbit.

HUBBLE TROUBLE
Launched from the shuttle in 1990, the *Hubble Space Telescope* was repaired by a shuttle crew in 1993.

The capture and re-deployment of the *Intelsat VI* satellite required a spacewalk of 8 hours 29 minutes.

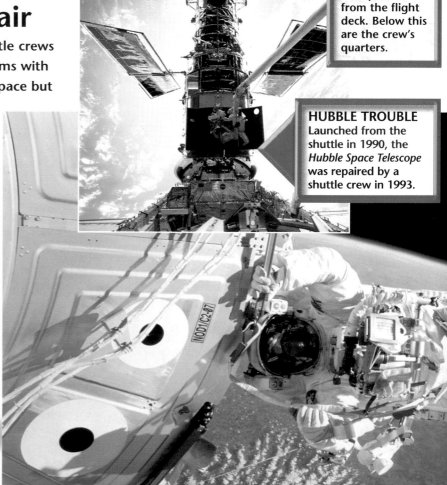

DATABANK

INPUT

Q Who is the oldest person to have travelled into space?

Q How many crew does a typical space shuttle mission carry?

Q What happened to the shuttle *Challenger*?

OUTPUT

A John Glenn, aged 77 aboard the shuttle *Discovery*.

A Usually six or seven.

A It exploded after take-off, killing its crew.

ROBOT ARM
Built by the Canadian Space Agency, the RMS robot arm weighs 411kg but can move cargo, such as satellites, weighing up to 29,935kg. It has a maximum length of 15m, making it the longest robot arm in the world.

SPACELAB
The Spacelab module provided 'shirt-sleeve' conditions in which a host of experiments could be carried out.

Spacelab

Spacelab was a re-usable space laboratory that operated within the cargo bay of a space shuttle. It was used on more than 25 space shuttle missions, almost a quarter of all shuttle flights, after its first launch in 1983. It was made up of a series of interchangeable modules. Some of these were pressurised and acted like an additional shuttle crew cabin so that astronauts could work in regular clothing rather than pressurised spacesuits. In these modules, many microgravity experiments were carried out, observing the effect of almost no gravity on a range of living things from eggs to plants and bacteria. Other Spacelab modules were unpressurised and known as external modules or pallets. These contained instruments, such as telescopes and radiation monitors, which needed to be exposed to space. Different Spacelab missions used different combinations of modules.

The X33-Venturestar may replace the shuttle. It will feature more reusable parts and make missions cheaper.

Astronauts lose over a kilo of weight for every six hours of space walking as it is such hard work.

HANGING OVER THE EARTH
Many shuttle missions are involved with building the *International Space Station*. This involves dozens of space walks.

FACTS AND FIGURES

The space shuttle orbiter is 37m long, 17.4m high and has a wingspan of 24m. It weighs 84,778kg.

The space shuttle weighs a fraction of a train engine but delivers as much power as 39 locomotives.

Each of the space shuttle's solid rocket motors burns 5 tonnes of propellant per second.

Unlike early missions, the space shuttle offers a varied food menu that is only repeated every seven days.

Weightlessness means that the crew must exercise for two hours each day to keep muscles and heart healthy.

Crew members must clean the shuttle every day to avoid a build up of potentially dangerous dust.

LIVING IN SPACE

During the 1960s, manned missions into space were short.
The arrival of semi-permanent space stations orbiting Earth
has enabled people to spend more time in space,
often conducting intriguing experiments.

Salyut, Skylab and Mir

The Russian *Salyut* and American *Skylab* space stations proved that people could stay in space for long
periods even though weightlessness had some effects on blood circulation and muscle wasting.
Salyut and *Skylab* each had one docking port to receive
incoming space flights. The *Mir 1* space station, launched
in 1986, has six. These allowed different craft and modules to
be joined with *Mir*, making it the largest structure in space.
Although plagued by problems, *Mir* was a success in many ways.
It set new records for long
stays in space and
paved the way for
the *International
Space Station (ISS)*.

There are plans to offer a short
stay on *Mir* as a grand prize on a
future TV game show.

SKYLAB
The USA's first space
station, *Skylab* was
launched in 1973 and
was built from parts of
a Saturn 5 rocket.

International Space Station (ISS)

The *ISS* is being pieced together by crews and flights
from the space shuttle and Russian rockets.
It will hold seven crew when
complete. Its massive arrays of solar
cells covering almost 4,047 sq m will
generate 110kw of power. The *ISS* will perform
dozens of experiments in its six laboratories,
looking at the effects of microgravity on cells
and living organisms as well as developing
new materials and industrial
processes which could
have great benefit
on Earth.

ISS OVERHEAD
The first section
of the *ISS* was
launched in 1998.
It will take a total
of between 44
and 46 missions
to complete the
88.4m long space
station. This
picture shows
what the finished
station may
look like.

The *ISS* spacesuit used for EVAs can be used 25 times before it must be returned to Earth for servicing.

Extra-vehicular activity

Trips outside of the craft, either to deploy a satellite from a space shuttle's cargo bay, or to work on a craft or space station are called Extra Vehicular Activity or EVAs. For these, astronauts need a spacesuit (see below), which protects them from harmful radiation, extreme temperatures and micrometeroids – fast-moving dust particles that could tear through regular clothing – and flesh. The space shuttle's Extravehicular Mobility Unit (EMU) is a suit made of many different layers of material, and is equipped with a main and reserve oxygen supply, half a litre of drinking water, a urine collection device and climate control. The suit weighs over 48kg on Earth and takes 45 minutes to put on. Astronauts wearing the EMU suit can work outside in space for up to seven hours.

JET PACK
The Manned Manoeuvred Unit (MMU) is a backpack featuring jet thrusters that allow astronauts to move around in space.

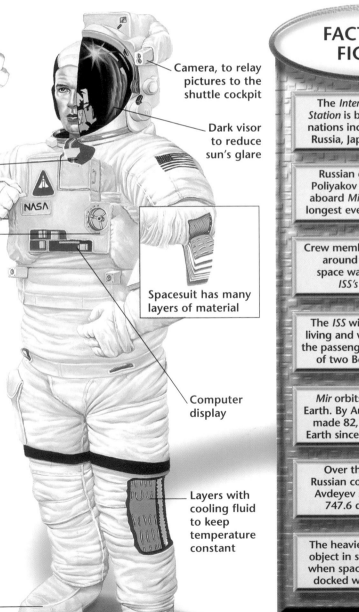

- In-suit drinking bag
- Glove – tailored for each astronaut
- Temperature control valve
- Camera, to relay pictures to the shuttle cockpit
- Dark visor to reduce sun's glare
- Spacesuit has many layers of material
- Computer display
- Layers with cooling fluid to keep temperature constant
- Boots – weighed down to counter weightlessness

DATABANK

Q Which was the world's first operational space station?

A The Russian *Salyut 1* was launched in 1971. It was visited by one astronaut for 23 days.

Q How will rubbish and waste that cannot be recycled be disposed of on the *ISS*?

A It will be returned to Earth or placed in a vehicle designed to burn up in the atmosphere.

FACTS AND FIGURES

The *International Space Station* is being built by 16 nations including the USA, Russia, Japan and Britain.

Russian doctor Valeriy Poliyakov spent 437 days aboard *Mir* 1994–95 – the longest ever space mission.

Crew members will perform around 850 hours of space walks during the *ISS's* assembly.

The *ISS* will have as much living and working space as the passenger compartments of two Boeing 747 jets.

Mir orbits 390km above Earth. By August 2000 it had made 82,150 trips round Earth since it was launched.

Over three missions, Russian cosmonaut Sergei Avdeyev spent a total of 747.6 days in space.

The heaviest human-made object in space, so far, was when space shuttle *Atlantis* docked with *Mir* in 1995.

SPACE PROBES

Space probes are designed to leave Earth's orbit and head out into space to explore, measure and send back information about other parts of the Solar System and potentially, the Universe beyond.

Better than humans

While humans are very adaptable, we cannot survive in space without tonnes of equipment. Probes are smaller and cheaper to build than manned spacecraft because they don't need crew quarters, safety systems and vast supplies of oxygen, water and food. What is more, it is easier to protect mechanical and electrical parts than humans from the radioactivity, toxic chemicals and extreme pressures and temperatures found on many of the Solar System's planets. Most probes are launched with no hope of return – an unthinkable mission for people.

Probes to Mars have a high failure rate. At least a dozen Russian and American missions have ended in disaster.

GIOTTO
The probe *Giotto* came within 600m of Halley's Comet in 1986 and sent a wealth of data back to Earth.

Orbiters and fly-by probes

Probes are often classed according to whether they orbit, fly by or land on a planet or satellite. Lander probes grab the headlines with their images of a planet surface beamed back to Earth, but probes like *Galileo* which went into orbit around Jupiter in 1995, have revolutionized our knowledge of the planets and space. One of the oldest fly-by missions is still considered the most spectacularly successful. Launched in 1977, *Voyager 1* is not only still working but will continue to do so until its power fails in about 2020. *Voyager* completed its main mission with a final fly-by of Neptune in 1989 but is now well into its second task called the Voyager Interstellar Mission. This is designed to investigate features of the outer Solar System such as its magnetic field and solar wind.

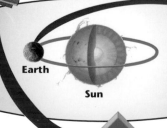

Earth

Sun

Jupiter

BY JUPITER
Galileo needed a slingshot launch (see right) to reach Jupiter. It used the gravity of Venus and then Earth twice.

SLINGSHOT LAUNCH
A space probe's speed can be increased or its direction changed by using another planet's gravity as a free-energy source.

On the surface

Few landers have the ability to move from their position, but a small number of amazing robots have managed to trundle around a small part of the Moon's or another planet's surface. The first of these were the *Lunokhod* robot rovers. These landed on the Moon in 1970 and 1973 and were driven by remote control from Earth. In 1997, the *Pathfinder* probe opened its petal-like panels and released the *Mars Sojourner* robot rover onto the surface of Mars. *Sojourner* was very successful in navigating its own way around the surface on its six wheels, analysing rock and soil samples and relaying the information back to *Pathfinder*, which then sent it back to Earth.

The *Pioneer Venus Orbiter* and *Multiprobe* were part of the same mission but were launched separately in 1978.

MULTIPROBE
The *Venus Multiprobe* released one large and three smaller craft to test the planet's surface and atmosphere.

LUNOKHOD
In preparation for putting a man on the Moon, the Russians sent two *Lunokhod* rovers to explore the lunar surface. These fragile vehicles sent back important data, but a Russian manned mission never took place.

The European Space Agency's Rosetta Mission will feature two probes. It will investigate a comet for two years.

STAY OR GO?
The first probe to land on Mars was *Viking 1* in 1976. It could not move around but sent back amazing pictures of the planet's surface (left). In 1997, the *Mars Sojourner* robot (above) could move around short distances. Its six wheels had studs for extra grip.

DATABANK

Q Which was the first space probe and where did it go?

A The Russian-built *Luna 2* successfully impacted with the Moon's surface in 1959.

Q How many space probes are planned to be launched in the future?

A In the next 10 years 45–50 probes will visit planets, comets, asteroids and deep space.

PIONEER VENUS LANDER
The large lander, 1.5m wide, performed seven science experiments. It did not survive on Venus' harsh surface for long.

THE FUTURE IN SPACE

Since the first missions into space 40 years ago, we have built up an enormous knowledge of the Universe. The future is likely to see many more such exciting projects that will greatly increase our understanding.

 ## New findings

By visiting places yet to be closely examined, future space probes and missions will help fill in some of the gaps in our knowledge of the Solar System. For example, from around 2009 onwards, the *Pluto-Kuiper Express* will examine Pluto and the far reaches of the Solar System. Other probes will focus even further afield. NASA's *Terrestrial Planet Finder (TPF)* will search for, map and measure the characteristics of planets orbiting nearby star systems. It may even locate planets with conditions suitable for life.

It is difficult for people to travel out of the Solar System because of the vast distances involved.

 ## Are we alone?

We are fascinated by the possibility of intelligent life existing elsewhere in the Universe. The Search for Extraterrestrial Intelligence (SETI) organisation monitors millions of radio signals we receive from the Universe, searching for a pattern, which may indicate the presence of intelligent life. It is a vast, ongoing task that may never reveal alien life. Yet many scientists find it hard to believe that throughout the entire Universe, life only exists on our small planet located on the outer edge of a modest-sized galaxy.

EARTH IS OURS
Many films have portrayed aliens as evil monsters in huge space ships eager to take over Earth.

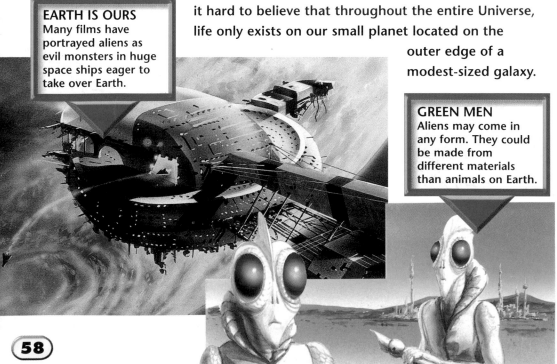

GREEN MEN
Aliens may come in any form. They could be made from different materials than animals on Earth.

FACTS AND FIGURES

NASA's *Terrestrial Planet Finder* will be launched in 2011, two years after its *Next Generation Space Telescope*.

The dangerous debris from space rockets that orbit Earth may be removed by a special laser blasting device.

Future spacecraft may have sails to harness the power of the solar wind. This travels at up to 900 km per second.

Current Mars missions include *Mars Surveyor 2001 Orbiter* and Japan's *Nomozi*, which will arrive in 2003.

In 2003, NASA will send a pair of advanced rovers to Mars to search for signs of water. Each has 10 cameras.

To be launched in 2008, the *Laser Interferometer Space Antenna (LISA)* will hunt for black holes in distant galaxies.

New crystal materials for industry may be manufactured in the microgravity of space.

SPACE MINERS
As Earth's natural resources are used up we may be forced to mine asteroids or try to beam down solar power from space.

People on Mars

Although it appears pretty certain that the red planet doesn't contain life at present, this is unlikely to stop a future manned mission there. The next wave of missions to Mars will include unmanned probes which collect samples and return to Earth. These could be launched near the end of this decade. Before a manned mission is attempted, unmanned probes and robots would have to be landed in advance to set up some of the equipment vital to a Mars colony mission. These robots could build living quarters and even start to produce fuel.

NEW VENTURE
Astronauts on Mars will need lightweight spacesuits as the planet's gravity is greater than that of the Moon. Energy is likely to be provided by solar panels, fuel cells and maybe even nuclear reactions.

It would take today's spacecraft at least six months to a year to reach Mars.

Return to the Moon

It seems likely that, in a generation from now, there will be a human presence on the Moon. With no atmosphere and interference caused by millions of Earth radio signals, it would be the ideal place for an observatory with both radio and optical telescopes. It could also become a staging post for deep space missions with craft launched more efficiently from its low gravity surface. Mineral deposits may attract lunar prospectors whilst the thrill of entering space may see small numbers of Moon tourists by 2040.

The Moon's south pole is a likely site for a base as it receives constant sunlight, providing endless solar power.

Terraforming

Terraforming is the changing of another planet's environment to allow animals, plants and humans to live there. Terraforming Mars would involve finding water, importing millions of micro-organisms adapted for life on Mars and generating vast amounts of atmospheric gases to trap heat and warm the planet's surface. The process would take many thousands of years but may be attempted in the distant future.

MOVING ON FROM EARTH
Any settlements on the Moon or other planets would have to be built from materials found on the planets themselves.

GLOSSARY

This section explains some of the more unusual or difficult terms that have been used in this book. The entries are arranged in alphabetical order.

ORBIT
The path of a satellite or moon around a planet. The time it takes to complete one orbit is called the orbital period.

Absolute magnitude The measure of the real brightness of an object. It measures a star's brightness as if viewed from 32.6 light years away.

Acceleration The rate of change in the velocity of a moving object.

Active galaxy A galaxy with a large black hole at its centre, which generates huge amounts of energy.

Apparent magnitude A measure of how bright a star appears to us on Earth.

Asteroid A rocky body in the Solar System a few hundred kilometres or less in size.

Atmosphere The layer of gas surrounding a planet or moon.

Atom The smallest part of an element containing subatomic particles called electrons, protons and neutrons.

Binary star Two stars in orbit around each other.

Black hole An object in space with such a strong gravitational pull nothing can escape it.

Brown dwarf A failed star that did not get hot enough for core nuclear fusion to take place to create a proper star.

BIG BANG
The theory that an immensely violent event billions of years ago gave birth to all the matter in the Universe.

Cluster A group of stars or galaxies that affect each other by their gravitational attraction.

Comet An object made of dust and ice. When its orbit brings it close to the Sun, some ice melts and creates a long tail in the sky.

Constellation A collection of stars grouped in an area of the night sky as viewed from Earth.

Dark matter Matter known to exist but invisible – believed to make up much of the Universe.

Electromagnetic waves Waves made of vibrations of constantly changing electrical and magnetic fields, such as light.

Electron A subatomic particle carrying a negative charge.

Escape velocity The speed at which an object must travel to escape another object's gravity.

Extraterrestrial Anything that originates or is located outside of Earth or its atmosphere.

Galaxy A collection of millions or billions of stars, planets, gas and dust bound together by gravity.

Gravity The force of attraction between objects.

Greenhouse Effect The warming of a planet's atmosphere as heat from the Sun is trapped by a layer of gas, such as carbon dioxide.

Infrared radiation A form of invisible electromagnetic radiation.

Light year A measure of distance, it is how far light travels in one Earth year – 9,460,700,000,000km.

Luminosity A measure of how much light and heat a star gives out.

Magnetic field The area around a magnet in which magnetic force works. Planets can act as magnets.

Mass The amount of material in an object.

Meteorite A large meteor that impacts with Earth's surface.

Meteoroids Small rocky objects in space seen only when they burn up in Earth's atmosphere as meteors.

Neutrino A particle with no electrical charge or mass.

Neutron An uncharged subatomic particle.

Neutron star A collapsed star made up mainly of neutrons. Small in size, neutron stars have an extremely high mass.

Nuclear fusion When two atomic nuclei produce a new nucleus. This releases a large amount of energy.

Nucleus (plural: nuclei) The protons and neutrons found at the core of an atom.

Oort Cloud A cloud of comets at the edge of the Solar System.

Pressure The force exerted over a specific area by a gas, solid or liquid.

Proton A subatomic particle that has a single positive charge.

Pulsar A spinning neutron star that sends radiation out into space.

Quasar A distant galaxy releasing enormous amounts of energy from a small central core.

Radiation Electromagnetic energy that travels in waves – given off by radioactive substances.

Red giant A bright red star up to 100 times the size of the Sun, believed to be at the end of its life.

Redshift An apparent increase in wavelength (becoming more red) of the light waves emitted from an object moving away from the observer.

Rotational period The time it takes a planet or star to rotate on its own axis.

Satellite An object that orbits another body. Includes man-made satellites.

Solar wind The stream of particles ejected from the Sun into space.

Supernova The explosive death of a massive star once it has used up all its nuclear fuel.

Ultraviolet radiation A form of invisible electromagnetic radiation.

Velocity An object's speed, which is calculated by dividing the distance it has travelled by the time it took to travel the distance.

White dwarf A hot, very dense, compact star.

X-rays A form of electromagnetic radiation that can pass through solid objects.

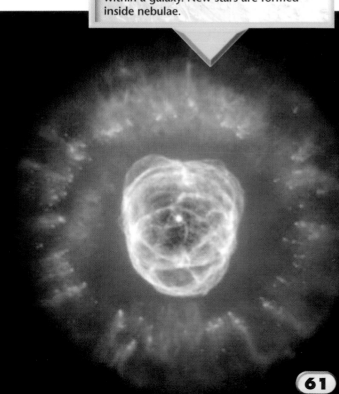

NEBULA (PLURAL: NEBULAE)
A large cloud of dust and gas found within a galaxy. New stars are formed inside nebulae.

INDEX

ACKNOWLEDGEMENTS

The publishers would like to thank the following:

 ## Photographs

 ## Artists & contributors

p9(cr) NASA; p11(bl) NASA; p12(cl & tr) NASA; p14(cl) NASA; p15(bl) NASA; p19(cl) NASA; p20(cr) NASA; p21(bc) NASA; p22(tr & cr) NASA, (cl) Science Photo Library/John Sanford; p26(tl) NASA/Jeff Hester & Paul Scower (Arizona State University); p28(tr) NASA; p30-31(tl-br) Science Photo Library/David A Hardy; p31(tr) Science Photo Library/Chris Butler; p33(br) Science Photo Library; p34(cl) NASA; p35(bl) NASA/Robert Williams & the Hubble Deep Field Team (STScl); p37(bl) NASA; p39(tr) Mary Evans Picture Library; p44(bl) Science Photo Library/Francois Gohier; p45(tl) Science Photo LIbrary/Dr Fred Espenak, (c & bc & br) NASA; p49(bl & bcl & bc & bcr & br) NASA; p51(tr) NASA; p52(tl & c & br) NASA; p57(cl) NASA, (bl) NASA/Mary A Dale-Bannister, Washington University in St.Louis; p58(tr) Science Photo Library/Roger Harris; p60(tr) NASA; p61(bc) NASA/ESA/Andrew Fruchter/ERO Team (STScl).

Every effort has been made to trace and credit the artists whose work appears in this book, and the publishers apologize to those whose names do not appear below:
John Marshall, Ray Grinway, Richard Ward, T Hader, Nigel Quigley, John Ridyard, Ian Thompson, Gary Bines, Michael Roffe, Josephine Martino, Janos Marey, Lee Gibbons, M Saunders, Chris Forsey, Robin Carter, Julian Baker, David Russell, Guy Smith, J Matty, Jeremy Gower, Sebastian Quigley, R Hayward, Terry Gabbey, Ron Jobson Marion Appleton, Jonathan Adams, Tom Connell and Michael E Fisher

Design
Mik Gates